Naked
THINKING

Naked THINKING

Phil D'Agostino,
MEd, LPC-NC

TRUE DIRECTIONS
AN AFFILIATE OF TARCHER PERIGEE

iUniverse®

NAKED THINKING

iUniverse books may be ordered through booksellers or by contacting:

iUniverse
1663 Liberty Drive
Bloomington, IN 47403
www.iuniverse.com
1-800-Authors (1-800-288-4677)

ISBN: 978-1-5320-0598-5 (sc)
ISBN: 978-1-5320-0597-8 (hc)
ISBN: 978-1-5320-0596-1 (e)

Library of Congress Control Number: 2016915968

Print information available on the last page.

iUniverse rev. date: 11/09/2016

CONTENTS

PREFACE

The concept of naked thinking is the product of my twenty-five years of helping my therapy and business clients apply the same principles of cognitive-behavioral therapy to solve their problems and become more effective in their lives. Each time a client brought an issue to me, I found that naked thinking showed itself to be the fastest and most effective way to overcome even the worst-case problem.

Naked thinking is thinking with the suffocating cloak of emotions stripped away. It isn't that emotions are bad, but when it comes to sorting out difficulties or making decisions, emotions can change the way you think so dramatically you often can't think at all, or what you do decide to do looks very different a short time later, once the emotion of the moment has passed. And, of course, the emotions of that moment always do pass, and that's when you get a chance to evaluate what you said, did, or decided. In many cases, that means that you now have to deal with the outcome and it's too late to undo what you've already done.

Whether it was helping people improve their relationships, be able to more confidently present themselves to bosses or groups, be better witnesses for legal procedures, or just have greater success overcoming anger, depression, or anxiety, these principles, applied in a less psychological and more practical context, yielded the best and fastest results.

Over time, it gradually became clear that the process was relatively the same and could be boiled down to specific steps to access naked thinking and live a life more by design than by chance. These steps coalesced into a process that can be taught, learned, and practiced, and they are presented here.

What makes this book different from others is that I use real-life examples and plain language to describe and illustrate exactly how to tame your emotions so you can focus your abilities and become more effective in decision making and implementation. While I do outline and explain these principles fully in such chapters as "The Perfect

Principle" and "The Naked-Thinking Bully Barrier" and others, *Naked Thinking* isn't meant to be a psychology book or even a psychology primer. Rather, the stories and exercises in *Naked Thinking* are meant to make these principles practical and relevant in almost any setting. And, perhaps most importantly, they include the critical elements of being immediately applicable, uncomplicated, and memorable. There is little value in knowing concepts or strategies if they are so complex or obscure you can't use them when you need them.

Additionally, when you begin using these concepts and methods, you will find that you become better able to take on life's challenges with a new sense of confidence. This greater sense of confidence frees you to be more open to new things and accepting of a broader array of experiences and relationships without fear. You'll be better able to fight your depression or anxiety. You'll be able to present your ideas more boldly and be a better leader, parent, or friend. In short, you will be better able to be the best you you already are.

Designed primarily as a step-by-step handbook to help ordinary people find a way to be happier and more effective in daily living, this book also can be effectively incorporated into psychology and social work, marriage therapy, leadership development, trial-witness preparation, management training, and other training programs. It can serve as a library or desk reference for professionals and nonprofessionals alike who wish to improve their own skills or those of others in focusing more and feeling less.

INTRODUCTION

How many of the following phrases have you heard tumbling through your mind or falling from your lips, way too often?

- Oh man! I shouldn't have said/done that!
- I didn't mean it. I was just upset/mad/hurt.
- Sure, whatever you want.
- You know what I should've said/done?
- Boy! I am stupid / worthless / a fraud / fat / ugly / better than everybody else.
- I don't need anybody for any reason.
- I'm sorry!

How many of these behaviors sound like you?

- You never tell your boss your great ideas because you think she'll think they're stupid or your coworkers will think you're trying to suck up.
- You haven't started playing that new musical instrument because you know you'll sound bad to begin with.
- You said something very nasty to your spouse/mate/kid/friend/boss without thinking and later wished you hadn't.
- You know you have to get around to investing / looking for a new job / dumping your current beau / starting your new business, but you're afraid you'll make a mess of it, so you put it off indefinitely.
- You find yourself stressed out over everything that happens during the day.
- You have no energy left at the end of an ordinary workday and never get around to spending more time with your kids/mate/pets/parents/friends.
- You hate your coworker/customers so much that you spend a great deal of time focused on them, either ruminating in your

mind or talking about them to others, so you get very little done at work.

These are just a few examples of what you might experience when your emotions are running your life. Or you often feel angry, hateful, jealous, resentful, vengeful, afraid, or haughty, and maybe you even fall in love or lust very quickly and easily.

Over more than twenty-five years as a licensed therapist, life coach, and personal-development specialist, I have spoken to thousands of individuals about what makes them miserable and stops them from achieving some of their greatest life goals. Almost always, it boils down to this single startling fact: they know what to do and even *how* to do what it takes to be happier or more effective in their lives, but their own emotions stop them dead in their tracks. Once they think about it for a few minutes and come to realize it for themselves, they always follow up with "So what can I do about it? Can you help me?"

The answer is a simple yes I can, as I have helped thousands of others before.

I wrote this book to teach you, the reader, the very things I've taught them. Very simply put, if you diligently read through the material and follow through on the suggestions I make for using it in your own life, then you, too, will be able to tame your emotions, focus your thinking, and reach the success you've always craved. It doesn't matter if that means being a better parent, spouse or partner, employee, manager, leader, or anything else; the stumbling blocks are usually the same, and the answer to fixing them is too.

Is this book and learning to use naked thinking for you? It is if you want to do or achieve any of the following:

- live a less stressed life while lessening your depression or anxiety
- be more confident about presenting your ideas to others at work or in your profession
- make important decisions that allow you to become more financially independent and self-reliant
- better control your anger, being hurt, or how easily you cry

- be a great mom or dad with the kind of patience and demeanor you can be proud of
- grow your network of influence and friends
- feel more willing to take on new challenges and conquer your fear of failure
- be able to assert yourself and live as an equal in any relationship
- teach your children how to make good decisions and not be torn down by bullies

If you want to do any of these and a whole lot more, then *Naked Thinking* is for you!

Section 1

Section 1 accomplishes the following:

- Naked thinking is fully explained, along with specific instruction on how to use it to achieve your goals of taming your emotions and making better decisions.
- You will learn why naked thinking is important and how to find the courage and motivation to step outside your current way of reacting to life and becoming the master architect of the life you want.
- Areas of special interest and use are explained with step-by-step instructions.
- Opportunities for insights, ideas, and explanations are given in the "whisper boxes" along the way. Here you can personalize your copy to make it your very own handbook for life.

For online resources to learn more about various topics covered, please see www.NakedThinking.com/ResourceSectionI. This site will continue to be updated over time. If a question about anything you read in section 1 comes up, check there first. If you do not find what you need, contact the author at Phil@NakedThinking.com.

THE FIRST STEPS

If you speak when angry, you'll make the best speech you'll ever regret.
—Groucho Marx

A hot temper is the soil of remorse.
—Ambrose Bierce

What we feel and the degree we feel it is a combination of how our genetics built us and how our environment shaped us. What upsets us in our own culture, whatever that may be, is often dismissed as trivial or even silly in others. There are many factors that have worked together over our lifetimes to create the symphony of different emotions and emotional responses in our repertoire. Unfortunately, what that winds up being isn't always in our best interest. At any given moment, we are the sum of our history and experiences.

Fortunately, we are not like the rocks on the ground. We are not totally at the mercy of our environment or history. We can make decisions about what we do now, what we learn about, and how we will take on any given day. And that difference extends to our minds. Our minds actually do what we want them to do. For example, if you told yourself to think about an orange, you could literally close your eyes and see an orange. That also means it is within us to see misery or joy in whatever may happen to us—seek and you will find.

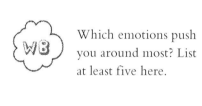 Which emotions push you around most? List at least five here.

Since we have within our power the ability to find in our lives both misery and joy, we can seize that power and become intentional about which we create for ourselves. Literally, we can choose to be happy (or happier, anyway) or miserable. But often we don't. Why not? What's stopping us? Why don't we just choose to be happy all the time? Based on my decades of experience as a therapist and coach, I offer these seven possible reasons:

1. What we decide will make us happy is too difficult to achieve or unachievable.
2. We don't know what to do or how to achieve those things that would make us happy that are achievable.
3. We don't know how to figure out or go about creating a game plan to gain or achieve the things that would make us happy.
4. We do know what might work, but it requires others, and we don't know how to get them to cooperate.
5. We do know what to do to reach our goals, but we cannot or do not make ourselves do them.
6. We have trained ourselves to be unhappy no matter what outcomes we attain and remain steadfastly committed to never giving up our justification to be angry, to complain, and to feel bad.
7. We don't accept the realities that are contrary to our goals.

Being happy doesn't come from nowhere. It starts with a list within ourselves that defines what it takes for us to be happy. We all have a list. Mostly outside of our conscious awareness, this list was developed over time and influenced by a host of variables like where we were raised, by whom, and other significant people and events in our lives. Most of us are unaware of the greatest portion of what's on that list. There are some in our lives that work very hard to put certain things on that list, and certainly the marketers in every imaginable medium work tirelessly to put what they sell on your list of "must haves or you can't be happy."

Since this list tends to be unintentional, it can contain some very disappointing elements. In fact, often we create an unachievable list of things we *must* have or do in order to be satisfied with ourselves.

What I mean is, as we move through our lives, many things influence what we think about the world and what would make us happy. We are taught what to believe is beautiful, tasty, fragrant, useful, and so on.

We are also influenced by parents, teachers, preachers, television, advertisers, and so on, as to what we should and therefore must have in order to be happy. For example, here in the 1950s, postwar America, we were told we needed the house with the white picket fence, the 2.1 children, a car, a dog, and a job to be complete and happy. Mythological? Perhaps, but many struggled to "keep up with the Joneses" in order to meet these ideals and achieve their expected level of happiness. And while that list is one we didn't deliberately make up, it still has a power over us. It tells us what we need in order to fit in, get along, and look successful. So a reasonable first step in taming our emotions and being the masters of our own emotional control panel is to review our list (to the degree that we can)

Admen play with your psyche!

There are many ways admen wheedle their way onto your list. Commercials for products are embedded in everything we see and hear in the media. News stories on the Internet are often really ads. Weekend radio programs with "experts" are often sponsored or paid for by people trying to sell you vitamins, financial products, or any number of gadgets. Over time, insidiously you find yourself feeling like you need to have one or buy one or at least look into it.

But there is also the more direct buzz for a new thing that makes it sound as though you are the only intelligent person on the planet that isn't doing it or using it, whatever the latest it might be. (Have you ever heard of someone camping out overnight to buy something when a store opens?) The result is a feeling called cognitive dissonance that acts as a silent pressure within, making you feel you have to have certain things or you won't be happy. Unfortunately, what you need is to buy it, not have it; so, often you wind up with many things you never use.

of what would make us happy, evaluate it, and perhaps change it. This may take some time, but it's an important use of time since this list is the underpinning of all of our happiness in the future.

For example, many of us believe we must have everyone's approval about everything about ourselves all the time. This, of course, is unachievable, and so we are doomed to have a diminished chance for real happiness. To many, the last statement may seem absurd, but I would challenge you to think about how you might feel if a complete stranger saw you doing something, came up to you, and told you how utterly stupid you seemed to him or how awful you look or dumb you are. Would you be indifferent to this person's statement? Would you become angry? Would you cry? Would you talk about this to someone later that night, like to your spouse or a friend?

The example is just one small way you might have a peek at your list. It shows that you do have a need or desire for continual approval even from strangers. While this specific issue may not be on your list, there are likely many things on your list of what would make you happy that are either completely unachievable or at least unreasonable. Being aware of that is the first step toward improving your chances of being happy in the universe in which you find yourself. And then once we know what to pursue, we need to figure out how to do it.

The Power of Courage

But even once we know what is on that list of what we need to be happy and even how to attain it, we also need courage. To me, *courage is the ability to face any strong emotion that leads us in a different direction from our intended goal, and still do the right thing regardless of how we feel.* Courage is that special something in us that allows us to deny an immediate pleasure for a longer-term gain or a greater step toward an ultimate goal. Courage is the single most important ingredient that allows us to pursue our plans with the chance of failure and still be happy if we fall flat on our faces. Courage is probably the most difficult of all the elements to find yet the most important to possess, because if you can't get past the emotions and do what you know will help, you've gained nothing. And part of finding that courage is to be willing to let go of even good reasons to be angry or sad and just choosing to not be, a very difficult thing for many of us to do.

Check out your list.

Use the space below to answer the following question as an example. Then use this same kind of question in different arenas of your life.

When I meet someone new, what specific traits, characteristics, or behaviors would I need to see before I would be interested in seeing or talking to them again? (You can use negatives like "not salacious" or "not political," but use them less than the affirmatives.)

Courage is found in the act of naked thinking. As we continue to explore these essentials to find ways to be happier and more productive in work and life, you'll be stripping away the cloak of your passions, taming your emotions, and focusing on the task at hand. You will see that, in decision making, thinking is more important than feeling, and changing the way you think is how to feel happier, less depressed, less anxious, more confident, and better able to withstand the challenges of life.

Feelings are a product—the end result of something we think (and therefore do). They are not the process or the means. To start with a feeling as a goal is to make you a slave to your emotions and vulnerable to manipulation. That is, if feeling is the be-all and the end-all of what you do, whatever drives a feeling the best at any given moment will be your motivator; and therefore, whoever or whatever dangles the promise of that feeling in front of you is your master.

An alternative title for naked thinking could be "Cogito!" In Latin, this translates as "I think!" or "I am thinking!" It's the source word for cognitive in our cognitive-behavioral approach. But Cogito! refers to something much more than the chemical processes of the brain that defines thinking. It means that I stop all else and consciously engage in that process that is uniquely human—the process of critical evaluation and decision making—before I act.

Stop reading and write.

As soon as you finish this section, stop reading and write down your questions, thoughts, criticisms, complaints, and compliments. Use them as a way to focus your purpose for reading further.

Certainly we all *think*, in that our brains are going through some kind of process like a car engine runs. Your brain is never off. It is always at least in idle, processing what comes in through the senses, and then we act in some way. This way or manner of thinking is usually the way we've trained ourselves over time to act automatically. Thinking is an action, even though it is unseen and internal. As a result, we rarely give a lot of conscious thought to most of what we do.

Our emotions color, cloak, and drive these processes. As we feel a strong emotion, different areas of our brain engage in our decision making. If we remain disconnected from this process by allowing it to be unconscious, it will be our emotions that drive us to act. Ultimately, when the emotion of the moment is gone, and it always goes away, we then have the result of what we did staring back at us. This is not the best time to evaluate that act. The best time is before we do it, and to make that evaluation stripped of the cloak of your passions—that is, with the power of bare-brained naked thinking.

Cogito! I Think— Therefore, I Can.

This does not mean, I think I can; therefore, I can. There is at least one good reason for it not to mean that, and that is it isn't true. It isn't true that you can do something just because you think you can. The cliché "whether you think you can or you think you can't, you'll be right" is just that, a cliché. There are things you cannot and will never be able to do no matter how much confidence you have. The emphasis in naked thinking is to *think* and not feel, especially when making important decisions.

More Focus Notes

The more and better you think, the more and better able you will be to know your true heart and create the goals that will gain for you what you find there. It is thinking that will allow you to create the plans and evaluate your progress. It is thinking that will permit you to accept the annoying, boorish, insulting, nasty, vicious, cruel, mean, and spiteful behaviors of others without those behaviors dictating how you feel or what you do next. It is thinking more and feeling less that will, once again, put you back in control of your own emotional control panel and get your own hands around your own destiny. Perhaps it is in your heart where your dreams are born. However, it is without a doubt in your brain, through careful thinking and planning, that your dreams can be actively pursued and brought to reality. But there is a catch. It takes more work, and sometimes we're going to be wrong.

What if we thinky-think ourselves day and night and devise great plans and pursue the plans with diligence? Does that mean we will always get what we want? Of course you already know the answer to that, but the reason isn't that you were thinking too much and feeling too little. It is simply that the world is full of unknowns. And while this is our greatest obstacle (not knowing for sure how to achieve success all the time), it is also one of our greatest sources of happiness. That may seem like a paradox, but this is the ingredient that makes life interesting. This ingredient is the uncertainty of life.

We rarely *know* what will give us a specific result when it comes to living our lives. Certainly, there are likely outcomes to a given situation, especially situations that occur commonly and in the same manner over and over again. But that is still a sucker bet! Unlike chemistry or physics, where you can map out a reaction and have a certain outcome, life is full of interacting variables. This is especially true when it comes to the complexity of interrelating the lives of the dozens of significant people in your life. For example, you may have had the same greeting at the door from your spouse for a decade, but today, somebody said or did something to her, and she is completely different. Like the old saying goes, "Stuff happens!"

But would you even want to know, with certainty, every outcome before everything you do? How dull and uninteresting life would be! Some might say, "Give me a little less interesting and a little more certainty." But they would soon tire of it. After all, if I already knew before I did something whether or not it would work or fail, why bother doing it? Sure, sometimes it would be great to know, but if it were all the time,

 All games and gambling is predicated on the thrill of not knowing what will happen. If you always knew the outcome of a friendly poker game or every shot on a pool table, what would be the fun of doing it at all? Money? After a short time, you might be able to make all the money you could ever spend, but then what? While it would be nice to know with certainty some outcomes in advance, knowing them all would make life little more than marking time until it's over.

it would make life very dull. It is this uncertainty that makes life hard and makes it worth living.

I cannot, and would not, do anything to eliminate all the uncertainty in my life, or show you how to eliminate it from yours, even if I could. It would be like eating of the fruit of the tree of knowledge. To bite into it would be to do it, be it, know it, and have it all, right now. Life would no longer unfold one wonderment at a time. Life would become unnecessary.

Uncertainty leads to victories and failures. That is neither good nor bad, though. It is not whether we fail to do something right or achieve every goal we set out to accomplish that matters in happiness. It is how we do it. It is whether we, in the process of the pursuit, remain true to ourselves—the kind of person we want to be in our self-image. Whether we remain true to our principles, ethics, and codes of morality during the process is what matters most when it's all said and done. It isn't whether we win or lose. It is that we *can* win *and* lose and that we are able to embrace each with the same joy for being in the game. *For without the ability to fail, there is no such thing as success!*

Tripping Down Our Yellow Brick Road

Naked Thinking is a journey of personal evolution and discovery—discovering what makes us happy, how to accept or change those things, and how to make them happen and accept the outcomes whatever they may be. It is a journey not unlike the journey Dorothy took in *The Wizard of Oz.*

Think for a moment. Dorothy was a little girl, egocentric with the expectation that everyone around her owed her the time and effort it took for her to have what she wanted. She was very much a person firmly in the "feel." When the movie opens, she goes from person to person to get their attention, and each in turn tells her that they have their own pursuits and she needs to move on alone.

Finally, feeling bad after her Aunt Em tells her she also is too busy for her, and a final push by Ms. Gulch, she takes up her little dog and decides to go off to where she will be the most important thing in the universe. Surely there is such a place. But where would it be? Obviously, somewhere over the rainbow—but how to get there? Not knowing, she simply leaves where she is (following the feel) to find what must be better somewhere else.

Once in unfamiliar territory, she begins to question (that is, to think more and feel less) her decision—but it's too late. Once her eyes were opened to herself as she was, she could never go home again. She tries to return but gets caught up in a vortex of self-doubt and self-absorption, symbolized by a twister. This maelstrom of egoism and feel-ism sucks her up and removes her from her reality and places her in the center of her own quagmire of unrealistic assumptions about herself, her home, and the people in her life—and she isn't in Kansas anymore.

In order for her to find herself and her way back to an existence within the realm of true reality, she must first understand herself and what about herself stands in her way. And so she begins her trip down the yellow brick road. Along that path, she faces those doubts about herself that have remained hidden from her. The scarecrow is her doubt about her own intelligence and ability to think. The tin man is her faithfulness to her dream and her fear or misconception that she may feel too little (and thus has no heart). The lion is the symbol of her own courage (the ability to stand up to her emotions and act responsibly), just out of her reach.

The path is also full of wonder and the hobgoblins of living, including the poppy fields, the emerald city, the flying monkeys, and the wicked witch. Step by step she plods on, not looking within herself but for some external force that will fix things for her. But what does she find? That the external force, the wizard, is just a man like she is just a girl. That he has his own problems that he is trying to fix for himself and that the only one that can make things right for her is she, herself.

Glinda, the good witch of the North, tells her that she had the power to go home and be happy within herself the entire time, but to tell her at the beginning would have been a waste of time. The reason is simple. She wouldn't have believed it, just as we don't believe it about ourselves.

What have we covered?

These are the major points we've covered so far. If you don't recognize them, go back and carefully review. Remember—we are exploring the fundamentals, and these points will be needed as we move forward.

1. Many things shape how we emotionally respond to our world, including our genetics and what we are taught in our cultural environment.
2. We all have within ourselves the means by which we can be happy, but something within us often stops us from being so.
3. We all want or need certain things in order to feel a sense of happiness or contentment. That list of things is often hidden and is sometimes deliberately created by others to motivate us to do as they would prefer.
4. The process of thinking more and feeling less when making decisions is the fastest and most reliable way to achieve that sense of happiness and well-being, and naked thinking is the best way to achieve that.
5. Achieving naked thinking requires a journey of self-discovery, and that may at times mean being uncomfortably honest with yourself about yourself. (And it never requires disclosing it to anyone else.)

WHAT WE'RE TALKING ABOUT

 Stop! Do this before reading this section.

Write down your definition of a good decision before you read mine. If, when you read mine, you agree or disagree, write down why. If you've never thought about it before, don't worry; very few have.

The purpose of learning and implementing the concepts in naked thinking is to tame your emotions and focus your thinking more, especially in the decision-making process. This allows you to make better good decisions. A good decision in this context is one that is consistent with your goals and ideals (morals, ethics, and self-image) and stands the test of time long after the decision is made. A good decision is also one that brings you closer to your goals. And finally, a good decision is one arrived at by doing your due diligence and sticking with a process that ensures you've considered every thing and every person relevant to the outcome. By making better good decisions, you also insulate yourself from the regret you may feel when the outcome doesn't go well—an unavoidable possibility whenever an important decision must be made.

But we don't make any decision in a vacuum. Every decision has to somehow mesh with all the other decisions we've made and make. Sometimes it seems that we are faced with incompatible choices. All of us want a lot of things at the same time, and as we focus on the most pressing on us at any given moment, it appears to be the only thing that matters or warrants our attentions. For example, right now you want to read these words and understand them. I assume this to be the case because you are reading them. Along with that, however, you want to breathe, be loved by special people, and so on. Also, you may want to be liked, to keep your job, to make money, to stay healthy, and to be a good person (however you define that)—and all at the same time.

But just because you want something very badly doesn't mean you would be willing to do absolutely anything to get it. You have limits as to what you might do, and those limits may be based on almost anything in your list of "other wants." Here's an example: You want a sandwich. But most likely you will not walk into a deli and shoot the next person you see with a sandwich in order to have one. Why not? Because, even though this would allow you to accomplish getting your desired outcome, a sandwich, the decision to kill stops you from having all the other things you also want, such as being a good person and perhaps staying out of jail.

The point is (and it is an extremely important point) that we all make decisions, but at times, the decisions we are currently making are inconsistent with other ideas and outcomes we want. As a result of making such a choice, we find ourselves thinking that we could have, and probably should have, done a better job at making that decision—making this a prime example of regret. But what drives us to make the decisions we do? What is that great impelling force that leads us in one direction or another? In many cases, it is our emotions.

Emotions are the root cause and effect of everything we do. In a very real way, they are the reason we do anything, for without them, we would never experience a want or sense of accomplishment. It's experiencing emotions like joy, surprise, fear, love, anger, confidence, and so on that make life itself what it is and therefore drives us to do what we do. Pick any activity. What do you ultimately gain from engaging in it? Whatever your answer, it will be a synonym for an emotion. It is the way we experience these emotions that helps us to develop personal preferences. Some of us prefer the thrill of fear (e.g., roller coasters and bungee jumping). Others prefer the feel of warmth and contentment (e.g., lying on a sunny beach or sitting in a room watching your grandchildren at play). But all preferences grow out of the different ways we each experience an emotion and the resulting desire to embrace or avoid it.

Without individual preferences for the various ways life can progress and the choices we make, reflected in our emotional responses to them, all our experiences would become neutral events. In essence, we would not care what happens to us or what we do any more than a car or computer does. But we are not machines. We are people. And so our emotions do count, and they are valuable. Just as they can at times be a blessing, however, they can in some ways be a curse. A machine will do as it is programmed or driven to do. We, on the other hand, will often stray from what we know is the best thing to do because our emotions, or

Monty! Monty! Monty!

Have you ever watched the TV show, Let's Make a Deal? One of the fun aspects of it is watching how people make their decisions to pick door number one, two, or three. In some cases, they want a prize so much, they doubt themselves, and the fear of making a mistake has them second- and triple-guessing what to do.

In other cases, they want to appease family members or friends that have been yelling which door to pick, so they are torn between whether to do as their spouse or their parent says.

In either case, they are being driven by their emotions. They get flustered because strong emotions change the way you make decisions. No matter what they do, if it isn't the big prize, they will always be able to say, "I shoulda picked the other door!"

anticipation of an emotion (fear), lead us, or all too often push us, in another direction. (The word *emotion* means to remove or forcibly move in a different direction.)

It is important then to keep our emotions in their proper placement in our lives. That is, it is of much greater value to stop elevating emotions to the level of a deity worthy of our worship and devotion and instead focus on our actions and realize that our intellect is what makes us different from other animals and enables us to live with honor, integrity, and intentionality.

It's All about Chemistry

The French philosopher Jean-Jacques Rousseau told us that if we feel it, it's so. For example, he would say if we feel something is right, it is right, or if we are afraid, there is something to fear. But how we feel isn't a matter of the universe speaking to us; it's a matter of chemistry. In fact, emotions are the results of just another of the chemical reactions that take place in the body due to the multiplicity of biological activities necessary to support and sustain life. Very often, these chemical reactions just happen and aren't really responses to anything; rather, they are simply improperly functioning or errant combinations of various elements in the brain. An example of such improperly functioning brain chemistry we hear a lot about is the feelings of being clinically depressed. Another might be a panic attack.

In the brain, electrical impulses are transmitted across the space between nerve cells with chemicals called neurotransmitters. An important example is serotonin. Since the brain cannot understand a constant stimulus, to make sense of the signal, there has to be a start and stop for each, creating a series of pulses like tapping a window to get someone's attention and not just laying your finger on the glass. It works something like a movie camera. As you take or show a video, there is a constant start and stop point for each picture or frame of a scene. Each frame is slightly different from the one in front of it, so that we see

Sound familiar?

"I'm sorry I made so much trouble for you with the boss this morning. I just felt you were trying to make some kind of commentary, but now I know you weren't."

"That's okay, but that isn't how I operate. If I believe a comment or opinion is warranted, I'll just say it."

As you can see, just because she felt it didn't mean her coworker was really guilty of her presumption.

change over time with each frame going by at a rate of fifteen to sixty different pictures every second. If there were no stops, all we would see is a smeary blur, and we would be unable to make any sense of it.

It's the same for the brain on a chemical level. Serotonin is sent from the tip of one nerve to stimulate the nerve next to it, creating a pulse or signal. But the pulse has to be short-lived so another pulse can be sent in rapid succession like the frames of a moving picture. As a result, as quickly as serotonin is produced, it is taken back up in a constant production/reuptake cycle. If the cycle is out of balance in one way, too much serotonin is allowed to accumulate, and there will be a "blurring" in the brain's understanding of the signal. If the imbalance goes the other way, too little serotonin is present to make itself known and actuate the next nerve.

What all of this means is that what we experience as emotion is a product of our chemistry, not of our decisions. Sometimes our emotions are consistent with and therefore deemed appropriate for what we do, but any number of things can lead us astray. Unconscious fears, cultural biases, a bad night's sleep, too much alcohol (some might say "just enough alcohol"!), drugs (legal or otherwise), and many other things can cause us to experience emotions that have nothing to do with reality.

An example of this is a woman walks down a sidewalk at ten o'clock at night. Without seeing or hearing anything, she begins to feel frightened. Following her emotion of fear, she steps into a diner and stays there for the next hour. She then continues to walk home without incident. Was she ever really in danger? Very likely, no.

Or a boy is riding a skateboard and finds himself at the top of a long flight of concrete steps at a park. Looking down, another fellow asks if he is going to skate down those steps as if daring him to do it. He feels quite confident he can do it without harm to himself. (Additionally, he could also feel angry at the question or embarrassed by the possibly implied message that he is being a coward if he doesn't.) His confidence high, although he never did anything like this before, he throws himself to the task. After six steps, his skateboard flips, and he falls, bumping and twisting until he lies at the bottom with a broken back. Was he really able to do such a dangerous stunt even though his emotion (pride, self-confidence, and other possible emotions) told him he was? The evidence is clear that he was not.

There is a real and insidious issue with using your emotional "gut" instinct as your guide. Our minds and memory play a trick on us. We remember the times when we had an intuitive hit (we can call that receiving positive reinforcement), and we forget all the intuitive misses (an indifferent event we have and dismiss dozens of times every day).

Charles Dickens, as far back as the 1880s, understood this simple concept. To illustrate how our sensations relate us to the real world, he places us in a room with a man and his conscience. In his *Christmas Carol*, Ebenezer Scrooge confronts the ghost of his long-dead business partner, Jacob Marley. Jacob, as a ghost, has tried to convince Ebenezer to change his future life-path. After examining Jacob's chains, Scrooge says, "Humbug!" to which Jacob responds:

"You don't believe in me."

"I don't."

"What evidence would you have of my reality beyond that of your senses?"

"I don't know."

"Why do you doubt your senses?"

"Because a little thing affects them. A slight disorder of the stomach makes them cheats. You may be an undigested bit of beef, a blot of mustard, a crumb of cheese, a fragment of an underdone potato. There's more of gravy than of grave about you, whatever you are!"

One could argue that Scrooge was wrong and Marley was really there, and therefore the author wants us to believe and trust our senses, our instinct or be emotionally intelligent. After all, Dickens leads us to accept Marley as a true ghost, and thus, Scrooge must be wrong for dismissing him as a byproduct of undigested beef. But by the end of that night, we have no way of knowing whether he really is a ghost or if Scrooge was simply in a state of mind that led him to reevaluate his life in a dream. Whichever it may be, the point is that even as far back as Dickens, it was acknowledged that our emotions are not to be taken at face value because even "a little thing affects them." The problem is that sometimes our emotional sensibilities are right, and sometimes they are dead wrong. In either case, they have very little to do with reality. They are a result of what is within us and not an indication of any reality or the world around us.

Naked thinking will help you decide where your emotions belong in your decision-making process, if anywhere at all. And if they are to be kept on a shelf somewhere until you're finished, our journey will show you how you can cut through the blue haze of your emotions and stay focused on your goals—regardless of how you feel. But there are those that cannot or will not accept that emotions and decision making don't mix. So captivated by the current cultural freedom of responsibility associated with being emotional, they will denigrate any attempt to diminish its elevated position in all phases of life and decision making. So let's anticipate their arguments and address each before proceeding.

The Myths about Being More Rational and Less Emotional

These arguments will at first seem to be logical and reasonable. On closer examination, you will find that they are simply myths that have been used to disparage any person or attempt to replace emotionality with clear and cogent argument (also disparagingly referred to as cold-blooded, coldhearted, mechanical, robotic, and steely; but approvingly termed professional, dispassionate, thoughtful, and deliberate). And this negative mentality toward bare-brained naked thinking is pervasive. There are scores of books extolling the greatness of feeling strong emotions and using them in your decision making.

These are the six myths we must address:

1. The point is to learn how to not feel anything at all.
2. Rational people believe that all emotions are wrong or bad and therefore you are a failure if you experience one.
3. To rational people, thinking alone is all that is necessary for a successful life.
4. When you acknowledge feelings at all or use words relating to them, you are inconsistent with your pursuit to more thoughtful decision making.
5. More rational (less emotions-driven) people advocate that it is always better to do what you think (believe) is right (or best) regardless of your feelings.
6. That's just the way I am. I can't help the way I am!

Myth #1: The goal is to learn how to feel nothing at all.

Thoughtful decision making isn't about feeling nothing, and it is not my intent to encourage or teach you to be emotionless. That is an impossible and unworthy goal. It's about being in control of your emotional state or taming your emotions. That is, feeling what you want and when, as well as how and if you show it to others. Some of the most emotional people on the planet simply choose to keep their feelings to themselves and just don't want or choose to participate in the emotional outpourings of others. It is important to understand and recognize that whether you choose to show or share your feelings with others or not, *experiencing a strong emotion can change the way you think and therefore influence the decisions you make.* Naked thinking is about helping you respond less to your emotions and think more and more clearly when making decisions, especially big ones. You will always feel something, and that's not a bad thing.

Myth #2: Feelings are bad or wrong and should be condemned as such.

Feelings are absolutely essential for making life worth living. In addition, no matter how successful you may become at controlling your response to your own emotions, you will more than likely continue to experience them. Thus, the point isn't to stop feeling but to be aware of your emotions and their effect on you. Some in psychology, legitimate and pseudo-psychologists populating daytime TV for example, argue that you are entitled to your feelings. The absurdity of the statement is that we need someone else's approval to have an emotion, or that we need someone else's support or acknowledgment when we have strong emotions. People feel emotions. That's just the way it is, and no one needs anyone's approval or acknowledgment to legitimize them. They are inherently legitimate on their own. The point isn't that you don't have a right to feel bad; it's if you want to make good decisions, maybe feeling less and thinking more is better. Neither is right or wrong, but taming your emotions and focusing your thinking may serve you better at a given moment.

Myth #3: Thinking is all that is necessary for success.

Not only is this not true; it is in reality the opposite of true. What I mean is that thinking alone (that is, only thinking and doing nothing else) is the one thing that can keep someone from success entirely. Some people think so much that at the end of a day they come to believe they've accomplished something great simply because they've done so much thinking! Neither experiencing strong emotions nor thinking alone is the way to be successful. Being a feeler is not an accomplishment; any animal can feel. Being a thinker isn't an accomplishment either; any healthy person can think. It is the actions that thinking generates that make the difference. The point of naked thinking is to help you find a way to shape what you do in a more meaningful and useful way. It is action that makes the difference and thus success. (Note: while another name for a person who yields to his emotions is infantile, a person who only thinks is a pipe-dreamer.)

The value of thinking isn't in the process; that is just the thinking itself. It is that thinking helps you to plan and evaluate the best approach to doing something. Ultimately, you must act, or your thinking is nothing more than a pastime or expense of energy that is no more constructive than sitting around feeling something. Thinking is a tool, a method, not the endgame. But since we feel so much so easily, and our actions tend to be automatic and consistent with our feelings, the emphasis of naked thinking is on using the power of thinking to increase the likelihood that our actions will produce the outcome we want, even after the emotion of the moment is gone.

Myth #4: You must abandon feeling if you are to endorse thinking.

The fact is that both thinking and feeling emotions are constantly present and a part of living deliberately. As a result, you cannot realistically speak in a "think" language that is devoid of references to emotional responses or taking action to make your thoughts become a reality. All three elements (thinking, feeling, and action … as well as a fourth important element, your self-image, which motivates your choices) are important in creating successful outcomes and a life lived with intentionality. As you progress through naked thinking, you will read stories that involve these four important elements, as they are all intertwined in life itself. In all cases and at all times, the purpose is to show you how to balance them in a way that is weighted more for success in the long run and not just to satisfy an immediate emotional need or impulse.

Myth #5: It is always better to do what you think (believe) is right (or best) regardless of your feelings.

This one is a little tricky. This myth says that the underlying premise is that you should always just suck it up no matter what and do the "right thing," no matter how distasteful. What makes it tricky is that the anticipation of the resulting feeling is one of the elements that may make what we do the "right thing." A personal example is my playing golf. I'm not very good at it, but I do enjoy an occasional "walk in the woods, with a little white ball as the excuse." I call it that because on a real golf course, I spend a lot of time walking around out of bounds in search of my little white ball.

One afternoon a while back, I had spent fifty-four dollars to play on a real PGA-rated course and another twenty-four dollars to rent a golf cart so my wife would go with me. (Who am I kidding? I'm a little lazy; the cart was for me.) In the rough on the twelfth hole, I hit the ball four times and only got about forty feet. My score was already over a hundred (a good game is less than seventy-two after playing all eighteen holes). Bored to tears and feeling very sorry for me, my wife asked why I didn't just quit and go home. I answered that I had just spent most of a hundred bucks, and I should finish. My thinking was directing me to believe that this was the right thing to do.

My wife went on. "Why did you spend the money?"

"Obviously because I wanted to play golf."

She then asked, "Okay ... why do you want to play golf?"

I answered, "Because I enjoy it."

"Are you enjoying it?"

"No."

In her own inimitable way, she had made it clear that the feeling of enjoyment was supposed to be the point of playing, not the activity itself. And since engaging in the activity wasn't yielding the desired result for being there, it made very little sense to continue. This is what makes myth number five tricky.

If doing a job (in the workplace for example) is so distasteful but necessary for some greater good, however you define what good is, then you must find a way to overcome the emotion and do it anyway. If doing a job is so distasteful and unnecessary, then use that fact in your decision-making process. A feelings-oriented person might just say forget it and quit. A thinking-oriented person might also quit, but he might decide to continue for some other reason, such as personal character development, to build work experience, or to make money while looking for other work. And it's this difference in why one decides what he will do that makes all the difference.

Myth #6: Feeling first or being emotional is just who you are, and you can't really change who you are.

There are branches of psychology that give credence to the idea that some people are more feelers than thinkers. There are many others that do not embrace this bifurcation of humanity and believe we are primarily a product of some genetic predisposition, and the rest, which is the overwhelmingly greater portion, is our upbringing. While it might be true that some of us are more prone to feel first and then think (I'm of Italian descent and can claim firsthand familiarity with the concept), we are still in far greater control over what we do and how we do it than a mere dog that salivates upon the ringing of a bell.

The familiar reference to Pavlov's dogs salivating after being trained to associate the sound of a bell with eating (explained in detail in "The Perfect Principle" that follows) is very apt here because many of us were similarly trained to feel anger, hurt, humiliated, and so on, when certain things happen. Proof that it's training is that over centuries or across cultures, people get upset or complimented over different things. That means it isn't intrinsic; it's taught. What that means is that if it's learned, it can be unlearned, and something new can be learned in its place—another fundamental element of cognitive-behavioral therapy. This isn't particularly easy, but to say "I can't help the way I am" is just not a true statement.

Keep in mind I am not saying that you aren't perfectly fine the way you are if that's how you want to be. But what goes along with that is if you remain the same and do as you did yesterday, you will continue to get the same kind of results you got yesterday. Our goal is predicated on the idea that you want something better (different) for tomorrow, so judging as good or bad isn't the point. Judging as to what is the most beneficial to your goals of happiness, effectiveness in your life, and so on, is what we need to look at. Once you've determined that a change is better, naked thinking helps you achieve it.

FOUR CRITICAL ELEMENTS FOR INTENTIONAL LIVING

Now that we've taken on the myths others use to stop us from being more think-oriented, we are free to develop within us all the elements necessary for successful, intentional living. Since feeling emotions is automatic and runs so much of our lives, this book is about developing the three other very important aspects of our lives: our thinking processes, our actions, and our self-image. Each has a role to play in living our lives with greater intentionality.

As noted, our thinking is best accomplished with the least amount of emotional pressure. Having strategies and automatic processes allows us to carefully evaluate and plan what may be our best means for achieving our ultimate goals.

Thoughts without action are wishes or pipe dreams where we metaphorically look into the puffs of smoke from our pipes and see in them our great fortunes and accomplishments never achieved, the way a child might lay on a grassy knoll and see giraffes in the clouds above. So I strongly emphasize moving beyond thoughts alone and doing what it takes to make the important things you want to happen, happen.

The last element we haven't talked about yet is your self-image, which is derived from your innermost beliefs about yourself and referred to by psychologists as your self-concept. How you see yourself and how you want others to see you is more than just a motivator to act; it's a motivator to *not* act. We often will stay away from certain activities because we fear that others will look at us and think things about us. Our image, either in our own eyes or in the eyes of others, is an important element in thinking more, feeling less, and becoming more productive. You can't really be a writer (your image of yourself) if you never write. You can't really be a nice person if you are never nice to people. You can't really be a (fill in the blank) if you don't do what these people do. If you continue to be or act in a manner that is different from or inconsistent with your self-image, you will experience what is known in psychology as a cognitive dissonance, and this dissonance is a cause of some types of mental distress and even disorders. Your self-image must be looked at, known, evaluated, changed, and supported in all you do, or your emotions will surely get the best of you.

The Basics of Cognitive-Behavioral Principles and Therapy

Naked Thinking is an approach to living based on the same well-studied principles as cognitive behavioral therapy (CBT). In order for you, the reader, to get the most from your use of this book, let's take a brief look at those principles. Knowing them allows you to see under the hood or behind the curtain so you can learn them, see how they are applicable in the naked-thinking approach, evaluate their effectiveness as you progress through the material, and apply them in your own life.

Depending on whose concept of CBT you read, there may be some differences in how those principles are discussed or identified. In this short discussion, our aim isn't to become expert academics in the nuances of the various ways they are used; rather, our aim is to be aware of the fundamentals well enough to make sense of them and be able to use them in everyday living. If you wish to become more expert, a simple Internet search with the following terms will yield very good results for your exploration: use "CBT fundamentals scholarly." The term *scholarly* will help your search engine weed out a lot of extraneous results.

Here are those fundamental principles that are most relevant to naked thinking.

1. **Staying in the present**. In any cognitive-behavioral approach, we would want to focus your attention on your current state. Going back to your childhood or trying to figure out how you got to be the way you are is of little concern. What is important is understanding where you are now with your situation, where you want to be next, and then how to get where you want to go.

    For example, in therapy, if you are anxious about speaking in front of a group, how that came to be may be impossible to determine and really isn't useful in what you might do to relieve it. It's about you now and how you are today; that will be your starting point.

2. **A C-B approach is goal oriented and problem focused.**
The point is to work on something specific. By doing so, you
not only take care of the issue or problem at hand, but you
are learning new ways to solve problems. Having a good and
reliable way to handle problems has the psychological benefit
of building your self-confidence (self-efficacy as explained in
"The Perfect Principle").

3. **The way you feel is connected to the way you think**. In
general terms, it's your interpretation of an event, not the event
itself, that causes how you feel. So monitoring your thoughts to
hear your inner self-talk is an important first step.

4. **Many thoughts are not based on reality and are harmful
to you**. When you begin to monitor your thinking, you may
notice how untrue some of those thoughts seem when you
actually begin to challenge them. One such type of harmful
thinking is the importance you give to some things that happen,
like a rude hand gesture.

5. **It's scientific.** That means you are willing to test any ideas
against evidence. In science, you start with a problem by
observing and analyzing it. You then create a hypothetical
explanation and test your ideas with the purpose of trying to
prove it wrong. (That's right. You try to prove it wrong, not
correct.) As you do this, you gather any new evidence that
might lead to a better alternative and accept what you find, even
if you don't like it. In naked thinking, some of the observations
we make are about ourselves, and sometimes we may not like
what we find. But this is about having a method of improving,
not self-criticism or punishment.

As you read on, you might see how these principles are incorporated.
It isn't important if you don't or if you don't give it another thought.
What is important is that you have what you need to move through
naked thinking with confidence and a sense of control.

THE PERFECT PRINCIPLE

Framework

Emotions play a central role in our everyday lives. Without them, we may as well just stay in bed. After all, what is the purpose of living if all it is is moving through one moment to the next until there aren't any more? Emotions are the mainstay of everything we do. Even the most ordinary, mundane, or primal of behaviors are instigated by some kind of emotion.

A quick recall of what you did today would yield a great number of emotions that stirred through you and then disappeared into the ether like they never existed. Granted, some of them weren't so nice, and some were so minimal you barely even noticed they were there—but they were. Along with that, though, is the occasional emotion that really sticks. You know what I mean—the really, *really* bad ones, and the really, *really* good ones. They can create quite a roller-coaster existence for many of us. For some, this roller-coaster existence is the allure of living and the very definition of passion.

Write down any thoughts that come to you as you read this section.

Many people, on the other hand, would rather there be a little less roller-coaster living and more glide-on-the-lake type of living. With serenity and peacefulness as the goal, they spend hours divorcing themselves from any emotional change through meditation or some form of it. To them, it is a kind of elevation of the spirit to a realm beyond the emotional. It is an escape from the worldly or the material. For them, to be able to do this is the attainment of an ultimate existence beyond that of being human to that of being one with God.

However you view emotions and the role they play in our daily lives for good or ill, there are some important characteristics about them we have addressed in previous chapters and a few we haven't talked much about. One characteristic of emotions we haven't really talked about is their origins within our minds.

Emotions, like everything else that happens within us, are nothing more or less than the results of our chemistry. Just like an ache, pain, or sense of cold or hot, chemicals pass along from one brain nerve cell to another until they land in a place within specials centers in our cerebral mass where they are interpreted and sent along to the cortex as thoughts.

These thoughts are considered both consciously and unconsciously, and emotions that are attached to these or similar thoughts are generated. During the process of considering these thoughts and feeling these emotions, new signals are sent, and those signals, like those just previously mentioned, then retrace the original steps over and over, creating a continuous feedback loop of thinking and feeling and thinking about the feeling and feeling about the thinking, and so on. This continuous feedback loop is critically important and never stops. Even when we sleep, it doesn't stop. It slows down a great deal, and we are made unaware of most of them during the course of our sleep, but they go on.

Sometimes these impulses begin from stimuli from outside of ourselves. Someone talks to us, and the impulse leaves the ear, travels down the auditory nerves, and the process mentioned takes over. A flash of light, a gust of wind, a kiss—all of these start the process, and then our conscious mind gets a chance to know it and consider it, evaluate it, like it or not like it, and so on.

Sometimes these impulses begin as mistakes. The chemicals in our body combine (or don't combine) when nothing happened to make them do so, and so they shouldn't have. Thoughts, feelings, and emotions can be generated for no reason except that the chemicals make them do so. For many of us, this can be the source of what is called a mood disorder; that is, some may experience depression or anxiety simply because the chemistry isn't working as it should.

These misconnections are the source of many issues within us, not just our psychology or mental state. We also get pain from nowhere, as in phantom limb syndrome, or feel hot flashes as hormones are readjusting, creating misconnections typical of menopause. Charlie horses, twinges, and twitches can occur as the various salts or electrolytes within us get out of balance. Since our entire body and being is our chemistry, when it works correctly, everything is as it should be. When it doesn't work correctly, it can create havoc so great it becomes the focus of everything we do.

And there is a third origin for these emotions we experience. As mentioned above, our thought/feeling feedback loop can begin from things that happen around us and we take in through our senses, such as seeing or hearing something. But the feedback loop can also begin with the echo from our past emanating from our unconscious mind, yielding a similar emotional state. And since it starts in the part of our thinking we never hear, we never know why we're feeling the way we do.

An example is that we might find ourselves saying to someone, "I really like talking to Jake. I barely know the guy, but there's something about him … I don't know what it is, but I just like the guy." A possible explanation for this can be that it is a type of transference first talked about by Sigmund Freud. Here what's happening is that your unconscious mind has within it a collection of feelings you have toward a person or people. When you meet someone who has similar characteristics, your unconscious mind interprets it as their being a part of that set of people and sends the emotions associated with them to you. Of course, all of this is outside your awareness, so you get that feeling or emotion but can't put your finger on exactly why.

Basic Underpinnings

This concept of transferring feeling or emotions already associated with other people or events from your unconscious mind to the present is just one way our unconscious minds have us feeling things without there being a way for us to know why we are feeling that way. There are many others. Another comes from the echoes of our self-image or sense of who or what kind of person we think we are.

To understand how this might happen, there are a few premises we must start with. The first is that the brain is in some ways like a tape recorder. While we may forget certain experiences, the brain still has them recorded. At this juncture, we must become very careful to not think that the brain is an infallible recording device and that everything is there and correct. There are many things that play into this recording. For example, we may mishear or misread the visual of an event; so if it does get recorded, it does so as the fact we thought it was and not necessarily the fact it really was.

But that's only one problem with the fidelity of the recording. Another is that, even if we hear it or see it correctly, our fears, biases, expectations, and our entire system of values will interpret it to make some kind of sense of it, then record it with that sense of it and not the reality of it. Consequently, at this point, we still won't know if what we recorded into our memories is accurate or a creation of our own thought processes in combination with the incoming reality, but it will seem accurate to us, so we will be reluctant to doubt our recollection of it because it fits so perfectly with our senses that it seems right. Eyewitness testimony and recall of "hidden" or "lost" memories, as in false memory syndrome, are notoriously unreliable for this reason. Witnesses will remain convinced they remember correctly even in the face of a video that shows that they are wrong.

Another premise we must establish in understanding how the echoes of our self-image can create our current state of emotion is that these recordings or memories have feelings or emotions attached to them, and these are very strongly bound together. What that means is that whatever you were feeling when you heard or saw something that gets stored in your mind gets stored with it as though it were part of the memory. An example is how good a jelly doughnut tasted when you were five and your grandfather would take you to the local bakery. You remember it fondly and tell your children about it. Then a day comes when you have them in your old neighborhood and take them to that same bakery where they still make those doughnuts with the exact some recipe. You all bite into one. Then your ten-year-old says, "Hey, Dad. What's so special about these? They taste just like the ones at the supermarket back home!" And you must admit to yourself that there's just no way to overlay your son's doughnut with your grandfather's love. The two will forever be connected.

Another example from an actual case is the imprinting of a TV personality's face during a rape. The person who was assaulted by a stranger in her own home turned her head away from the assailant while the TV was playing. She went into a kind of dissociative state wherein she sort of mentally left the room. When she began to renormalize after her period of shock, she became convinced that the person who was on TV was her assailant. This tells us that the mind is terribly powerful in some ways, very fragile in others, and decidedly unreliable when it comes to memory or the emotions that we might feel.

But there is another type of conditioning called classical conditioning. (Hang with me and just follow the definition, and I'll explain in a bit.) Classical conditioning is a kind of learning that occurs when a conditioned stimulus is paired with an unconditioned stimulus. Usually, the conditioned stimulus is a neutral stimulus (e.g., the sound of a bell), the unconditioned stimulus is biologically potent (e.g., the taste of food or pain), and the unconditioned response to the unconditioned stimulus is an unlearned reflex response (e.g., salivation or flinching). After pairing is repeated (some learning may occur already after only one pairing), the person exhibits a conditioned response to the conditioned stimulus when the conditioned stimulus is presented alone.

For clarity and to make this simpler to follow, let's go back to the turn of the 1900s. The famous Russian physician Ivan Pavlov presented this concept of classic conditioning to the world and showed how it worked with a group of dogs he had conditioned. First, he would ring a bell and then feed the dogs. When dogs eat, they salivate. So here we have the conditioned stimulus (the sound of the bell) associated with the unconditioned stimulus (the dog's food), and the unconditioned response happens automatically when fed (salivating). After associating these things together many times, Pavlov showed that the dogs would salivate without the food present just because they heard the bell; to their brains, that meant they were going to eat.

Now back to the real world of today. Do you have a dog or a cat? Have you ever seen them lick their mouths at the sound of your opening the doggie treats bag or the sound of the can opener? Without your realizing it, you have conditioned your pets. The reason they go to the bathroom so quickly when you let them outside is they are conditioned to need to go with your walking to the door or putting on their leash. If you put on their leash and get interrupted by a phone call, you may find they couldn't wait for you to finish your call, and now you have "Pavlovian Dog Evidence" on the floor in front of the door.

While you may find all this quite fascinating, you may be wondering why I'm telling you about it now. Well, if you are to fully understand, appreciate, and use the Perfect Principle, you must understand what's going on inside your own head. As stated in various places throughout *Naked Thinking*, the first thing we must do in problem solving and decision making is to evaluate whether we really need to do anything. Then we must gather all our information, beginning with a good understanding of what the starting point is. Our starting place for the Perfect Principle is the conditioning we've had and where our mind is as we begin our understanding of the principle itself.

The Setup

Many of us find ourselves unable to move past a certain level of activity toward a goal because we fear that we won't do something right. And by "right" I mean correctly. And by correctly I mean perfectly correctly without flaws and with perfect results the first time. As children, many of us were taught (or trained or conditioned) to feel stupid, awkward, or embarrassed when we did something that was either incorrect or different from the customs of our group.

This was reinforced many times through interactions with others we loved or respected or wanted to love or respect us. An example is a young girl hearing her mother and her mother's friends talking about the dress or hairstyles of another, or a young boy hearing a coach berate a teammate when he does something less than stellar. While these were deliberately stereotypical for clarity, the concept is experienced over a great number of interactions within a host of groups. Over time, we become imbued with the sense that doing something less than perfect in the eyes of someone you care about is a proper time to feel some kind of "bad." In fact, it may not just be a sense that it's proper to feel a bad emotion; it may be a sense that it's obligatory. Have you ever heard the expression "You should be ashamed of yourself"? In many cases, you're told to be ashamed for speaking up to a tyrannical teacher or deciding to wear something others don't like.

Once this begins to seep into our psyche, it also begins to create our mechanism for judging ourselves in our own eyes. After years of this imprinting, training, or conditioning, we no longer require the presence of others for us to feel bad about ourselves, even when no one else is looking or will ever know or be affected by what we are doing! In essence, we are trained by some to feel really awful about ourselves by remote control—and that person with the finger on the remote may even be long dead!

For some of us, this creates a sense of dread when we find ourselves in a situation wherein there is a chance for such self-evaluation. This is even greater when there is a chance for others to observe and judge us as well. An example might be the turning in of a report, or the presentation of our research or ideas to others in the workplace. This dread can become so intense that some go into a full-blown panic attack or become physically ill. Some experience anxiety so great that their response to it is to become depressed and sleepy, dull-minded and lethargic. It can be debilitating.

In psychology, we simply refer to this dread as anxiety. If that dread is pervasive—that is, it seems to haunt you whatever you're doing—it's called a "general anxiety" and can cause real physical manifestations like headaches, back pain, tingling sensations in the limbs, and a panoply of strange and diffuse symptoms. And while almost no one wants to feel this way, there is sometimes a reinforcement for feeling it. For example, if you are known to be a person who gets all upset with anxiety when asked to do certain things, others tend to not ask you to do them. In a real way, this is a form of reinforcement that can make it worse or even harder to shake off.

As a result of all of this, some people find themselves almost frozen with fear at the thought that what they are about to undertake might look bad to others or even their own critical inner-self. They procrastinate. They make excuses. They continue to research and analyze to be as sure as they can be that they won't make a mistake. And while they do so, they not only become ineffectual in what they're trying to do but look ineffectual to the very people they want to impress. Since one of those people might be they, themselves, they already feel like a failure and therefore feel that accompanying bad feeling, whatever it is.

The outward signs of this might be to become overly critical of others as a way of deflecting or redirecting criticism away from themselves to others. Another is to convert this emotion into a more active emotion so they can externalize it and "do" something with the emotional energy it produces. It can look like anger, hatred, jealousy, or revenge, or they might convert it into a long stream of doing altruistic things that might even be self-defeating in some ways.

This last example might need a little explanation. Consider people who are so concerned about their own "inadequacies," as defined by the echoes of their unconscious minds, they can never really get around to doing what they say they should be doing. As a way of compensating, they agree to do all kinds of things within their churches or the community. They volunteer to head up such projects as office parties and the like. They seem continually busy but just not at what they are supposed to be doing, as they say they should. These are the people who just can't say no. I know you've known some like that. In fact, you may be one of those yourself. It is a common way to deal with this issue.

The Principle

The common name for this psychological stumbling block is perfectionism. Let's define it a little better before we move to the Perfect Principle itself.

Perfectionism

In psychology, it is a personality trait characterized by a person's striving for flawlessness and setting *excessively* high performance standards, accompanied by *overly* critical self-evaluations and concerns regarding others' evaluations. It is a multidimensional characteristic, as psychologists agree that there are many positive and negative aspects to it. In its maladaptive form, perfectionism drives people to attempt to achieve an *unattainable ideal*. Their adaptive perfectionism can sometimes motivate them to reach their goals. In the end, if they reach their goal, they derive pleasure from doing so. When perfectionists do not reach their goals, they often fall into depression and enter into a cycle of never-ending self-deprecation.

In this definition, we see that perfectionism can be a stimulus for doing your best; but being motivated to do your best isn't really perfectionism. Perfectionism requires that your criteria for success are never really reachable, no matter how well you do. In fact, you may know people so anxious about their performance they cannot take a compliment without continuously asking you to justify the compliment, or they dismiss it out of hand. They may minimalize their achievement as an accident or compare it the performance of others as being still less than what they could have or might have or even should have done.

Here now is the paradox of perfectionism and my Perfect Principle itself:

Perfect Principle

All people do things that are, at times, wrong or bad. They learn by making mistakes and by doing things right. Their biases, wants, wishes, and sense of how things are supposed to be will make them continue to do certain things even after they know they are wrong.

Since all people do this, to do this (that is, make mistakes and do things wrong sometimes) makes one a perfect person. To not do this (that is, to never make a mistake or do anything wrong) is not what people do; so to never make a mistake or do things wrong makes you imperfect for being perfect, which makes you imperfect as a person. Therefore, to strive to be a perfect person would be to strive to make mistakes and do things wrong, at least sometimes. To strive to never make a mistake or never do things wrong is to strive to be a perfect person, which is then to become imperfect.

As you can see, to pursue being perfect is to pursue being imperfect! Now we must temper this a little with some reasonable thinking. When I say that to seek perfection is to seek imperfection, I do not mean the same thing as trying to create the best results you can when doing

By now, almost everyone will have some thoughts about the Perfect Principle. Write yours here. Include what it means to you, how it affected you when you read it, what you will now do since you've read it, and anything else important to you.

something important. If, for example, you are a surgeon and attempting to take out a cancer or do an organ transplant, you are definitely seeking perfection. Here, the perfection you're seeking to achieve isn't in being a perfect person; it's a perfection in the execution of the activity. If the person still dies, you may feel bad about it but believe or know you did everything you could. In another example, if you are playing the piano in a Tchaikovsky competition, you again are seeking perfection but in the execution of the piece, not in the self. There can be only one winner. At some point, you accept that and continue to work on your technique or just move on.

It is useful to focus on being good and doing your best or even better than your best when the stakes are high. It is when you are so afraid your best will lead to judgments from others or yourself about you as a person that you do nothing is what we're talking about. This inner turmoil and anxiety over making mistakes or being judged as bad or inept is the result of all the training (conditioning) you received from others and the reinforcement of it from your own inner voice.

Have you ever heard someone berate themselves because they said or did something that really was dumb? I mean, we all do dumb things sometimes, but there are people who then go the extra mile and really run themselves into the ground for it. I once knew a girl who would smack the top of her head and say things like, "You are so stupid! You shouldn't have done that! You're such an idiot! How stupid can you get!" And, of course, the litany of criticisms went on for a minute or more—at least on the outside. Insider her head, it probably kept on for hours if not forever. There are people who will remember every dumb thing they ever did, even years later, and this is a major reason why perfectionism can be devastating. It is a major component of the irrational or unrealistic thinking (or cognitive distortions) we want to challenge in cognitive therapy.

The Value of Understanding the Perfect Principle

There is a very important aspect of your self-image in psychology referred to as a sense of self-efficacy. Simply put, the term *efficacy* comes from a Latin word that means to accomplish or be effective. Efficacy is another way of saying that something has the power or ability to be effective in creating or accomplishing a specific result. When something, like a medicine, can accomplish the desired result, like curing an illness, it is said to be efficacious, and the measure of how well it can do it is called its efficacy. Self-efficacy is your measure of your own ability to accomplish what you need to in your own life.

We often hear people speak of something called self-esteem. When people use this term, they are usually meaning the sense of liking yourself, or loving yourself as some like to put it. Buried in a real sense of self-esteem, though, is the sense that you can do or accomplish what is important to you. It is a can-do optimism about yourself upon which stands your basis for self-confidence. Without that sense of confidence, you fear everything you might be called upon to do because your little inner voice is telling you that you can't do it and that you'll just make things worse if you try. And, of course, if you do try and do goof it up, as we all do sometimes, your little voice is there to reinforce your failing with the "See! I told you you'd goof it up!"

The value in knowing this isn't to sit around and have little intellectual chats with your friends about what's going on in the dark recesses of your mind. It isn't to be—or at least sound like you are—the smartest person in the room. The real value in understanding these concepts is that it gives you the underpinning for changing and taming your emotions, focusing your thoughts, and making your life one of design and not happenstance.

The way to use this information is to challenge these thoughts (cognitive distortions) about yourself and accept the fact, and again it is a fact, that you will at times do things incorrectly, make mistakes, look dumb to some people sometimes, and really goof some things up so badly you might need help to fix them, or they may never be

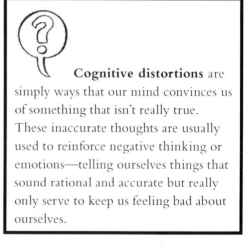

Cognitive distortions are simply ways that our mind convinces us of something that isn't really true. These inaccurate thoughts are usually used to reinforce negative thinking or emotions—telling ourselves things that sound rational and accurate but really only serve to keep us feeling bad about ourselves.

fixable! Does that sound awful? Well, it's not awful; it's just the way life is. Remember that the Perfect Principle begins with this as a premise of real life and real people—perfect people aren't perfect.

Applying the Perfect Principle

Acceptance of the fact that people are fallible and will make mistakes comes with time, practice, and reinforcement. Remember that the way you currently think and feel when things happen in your life is a matter of practice and reinforcement already. To undo and redo your thinking structure will require the same process. The good news is that this will happen almost automatically as you proceed with the next part, which is challenging the disparaging thoughts of yourself and substituting them with new thinking about your true ability to do well for yourself and others.

Challenging your thoughts about how awful you are must start with reality. The fact is you must be pretty good at most things or you wouldn't have even survived this long. Here you are reading a book that you found a way to buy, or you were able to create a friendship strong enough that someone wanted to give it to you as a gift. Even if you have a therapist that put it into your hands to read, you still have had the success of getting help. Again, the fact is you must be successful at some things or you wouldn't be here now in front of this book.

In the real world, however, most of us have more successes than just the fact that we have survived this long. My bet is you've done hundreds, if not thousands or tens of thousands, of really good things in your life. You may have graduated from a school or university. You may have fathered or mothered really well. You might have created something really useful at work or made a wonderful home life for your family. A list of possibilities is infinite really, because the number of things you might do at any point in your history was infinite as well.

Start with making a list of just a few things that you think you did really well. If your current thinking of yourself isn't particularly helpful, find someone who knows and cares about you. Ask your parent, spouse, kids—anyone that really knows you and may even love you—to tell you what they think if asked to list your accomplishments or what you're good at. They will have that list.

Things you've done well:

When you find yourself depressed or anxious, remind yourself of that list. Tell yourself the truth that you've done other things well and you can do this too. Remind yourself of the fact that you have gotten by this long and gone this far by your own pluck and determination. Even if others have had to help you along the way, you took that help and made something of it. If you are very accomplished, this will be even harder because you already know your strengths, and your inner voice has already found a way to discount them. You must be committed and persistent. You must do this every time you feel anxious, and I would recommend a couple of times a day even when you're feeling fine (further on, we shall call this success imagery). In a sense, you must wear a new path for your thinking, and like a new path in a meadow, you have to walk it many times to wear down the growth of your past.

The other thing you will want to do in applying the value of the Perfect Principle is to find a way to get over or accept things when you actually do goof things up. Remember people make mistakes and do things wrong, so you will too. This book or process will not eliminate the chances that when you do something, it might go badly. I'll give you an example of how silly this worry can be and how a person might handle it.

At a soccer game, a fellow in his late twenties was sitting on the sideline watching his kid play. While he was sitting there, he spilled his water bottle into his lap by accident. There was a break, and he needed to cross the field to talk to his kid while a few hundred people stood around the sidelines watching him do it. When he stood up to cross over, he noticed his pants and hesitated for three or four seconds. It looked—well—like his mistake may have been of a different nature. After his hesitation, he just walked across the field and took care of business. Did anyone notice? Oh, yeah. Did anyone make comments and laugh? Most assuredly. Did anything bad happen to him as a result? No. And here is the heart and soul of the matter: things will happen, and other people may very well think things about you that you won't like. But in the big scheme of things—so what? Practice this kind of inner strength like you practice getting things right (further on, we shall call this coping imagery).

Getting over it is important for your health and happiness. Sometimes, just getting over it isn't what the situation requires. If it's your boss who's seeing your mistake or failure, there may be greater consequences, so you need to make adjustments to be appropriate to the situation. But even your boss is a person who also makes mistakes or does things wrong sometimes. He or she will occasionally do something that could be a cause for ridicule. Remind yourself that you can get through it because you already know in the past you did get through it. To be perfect is to not be perfect, which makes you a perfect person.

Cogito! It is important to understand that the Perfect Principle is only one way our inner thoughts or self-talk can stop us or even debilitate us. Use the same methods here to quell that negative thinking and move on to better things. Specifically, do the following:

1. Listen to that inner voice or self-talk and hear what it's saying and the specifics of the negatives it might be enumerating.
2. Challenge that negative thinking with your list of what you know is good or better about yourself or what you can do.
3. Visualize (that is, practice in your mind) yourself doing things the way you'd like to see them go for you. This can be called "success imagery."
4. Visualize yourself making a mess of it and taking it in stride and how you handle it if things do go wrong. This can be called "coping imagery."
5. Practice or visualize this a few times a day (conditioning with intentionality and purpose).
6. Analyze what happened. When you do something that turns out badly, think through how to better handle it and practice that. If it goes well, add it to your list of what you know you can do as another proof that your negative self-talk is wrong.
7. Teach it to others. If you really want to learn this and make it as automatic as the current state of self-criticism your self-talk might be, teach this to someone else you know and care about. There is no greater gift than helping someone have a happier life.

In Conclusion

We all do things we wish we had done better, but perfectionism is an emotional trap. You can never be perfect, so seeking to be is self-defeating. Remember—since we are all imperfect in some way or other, being the imperfect person we are makes us perfectly who we are. Seek to do well, and when it's really important, seek to do the best you can. As the old adage goes, you can only do what you can only do. Embrace it.

DECREASE YOUR STRESS WITH NAKED THINKING

Sometimes it feels like the world just won't leave you alone. The bills keep coming. You're frazzled by the demands of life. There always seems to be something keeping you from just relaxing and doing nothing. Stress is hiding in every nook and cranny.

The good news about stress is that there are things you can do right now to bring down your level of response to it. You can manage it, and in some arenas of your life, you can even eliminate it completely. You actually do have more control over stress than you might think, but it requires you to step in and take that control. Stress management or reduction means taking control of what you do, think, feel, and how you respond to problems.

In the space provided, write down at least five things you think of as causing you stress. It can be anything at all, but be specific. For example, if your job is one you identify, find what it is about your job that bothers you the most. If there are several things in that job, write each one individually.

List at least five things that cause you stress.

individually. If you need more space than what is available in the whisper box, find the next available spot in the book and continue, making a note in the whisper box as to where it is so you can refer back to it later. For example, if you run out of space, you might find space you didn't use on page 32, so you continue your list there and put this at the bottom of this box: "see p. 32 for the rest," or something similar. You might also note "continued from page XYZ" on page 32 so you'll remember what this is in the future.

Keep these notes as specific as you can make them and avoid using a person or a name. Instead, if a specific person is your source of stress, write what it is he or she says and does that is the problem for you. Use behavioral language and stay focused on what happens and not who is doing it.

Finally, remember that this information is yours and may be confidentially yours alone. So you will want to be sure that you use language that makes sense to you and will in the future but is sensitive to the possibility that someone else may read it. This may not be an issue for you, but then again, naked thinking is about making decisions with a clear head and a look through them to what may transpire as a result.

Pick one of the sources of stress from your list to use as your working example. We will then apply the principles of naked thinking to analyze the situation and gain a greater understanding of what is the true cause of the stress you experience. Then we will have something to work with as you proceed through the steps below. To make it easier to understand, I'll give you an example, and we'll work through it together as you apply what we do to your own.

Teresa comes into my counseling office and complains of stress. She says that just driving into the parking lot at work causes her a great deal of anxiety, and by the time she starts actually doing the job, she's a wreck. The following conversation is used to tease out the elements in this story and find the root cause of the stressor.

"What goes through your mind as you pull into the parking lot?"

"Oh man! Here we go again—another day, another day of dealing with the drama!"

"Drama? You said you drive up and go into the workplace and start working. What drama are you referring to?"

"It's a long story, but it's all about Gloria."

"I've got the time. What about Gloria?"

"Every day when I get inside, all I want to do is get past Gloria's workstation and get on with my day, but she wants to stop me and go on and on about every little thing in her life. I don't really know her, and I don't really like her. I really, *really* don't want to know about everything going on in her life."

"So?"

"So I try to find a way to slither past her and get to my desk. But she lies in wait just to stop me, as though she knows I don't want to be bothered and is trying to make a point. The other day, she complained to our manager that I'm unfriendly, uncaring, and a coldhearted—well, you know the word she used. My boss asked me to be nicer to her. Me! He wants me to be nicer to her! I told him all I want is to do my job and go home. But he said that I have a responsibility to be liked and get along with others. I guess I'm supposed to understand them and accommodate them, but they don't have to leave me alone if that's what *I* want!"

Here we now have what's really bothering her. It isn't her work. It seems to be that she feels powerless to control her own work environment while others, particularly Gloria and her manager, get to control theirs and hers as well. For Teresa, there is an injustice, and she won't allow herself to just accept that some people will go out of their way to impose themselves on others. In her follow-up, she said that she shouldn't have to. She should be able to just get on with her work and be left alone. Her boss should stand up for her and tell Gloria to leave her alone in the mornings.

If you read carefully, you will note that Teresa's issue is that the world isn't conforming to her demands on it. Her litany of "shoulds" is continuously rambling through her mind, and this is the cause of her stress. Using naked thinking allows us to cut through all the feelings and find the real issue. In this case, it's a sense of disloyalty from her manager and a belief that she isn't being treated as fairly as she thinks she should be. It is these demands (i.e., that the world should treat her as she believes it should) that are the root cause.

If you identify with Teresa, you may also experience an empathetic twinge of her angst. But consider this: Jennifer has also been working there for five years, and Gloria does the same thing to her. Teresa asked how she can seem so bubbly in the morning, and she told her that it's because she decided a long time ago that it just wasn't worth it to get upset over what Gloria does. When Teresa asked if that means Gloria "just gets away with it," Jennifer said that that is one way to look at it. Her way to look at it was to see Gloria the same way she sees traffic—just the way things are on the way to work.

Analyze the elements in your own example now. Go through it and ask yourself questions like the following:

- What exactly happens or happened?
- Who did it or said it?
- If someone else said or did it, would it still bother you as much?
- What was actually said, verbatim not paraphrased?
- What is it about that or the situation that bothers you?
- What is it about what bothers you that bothers you (as in, why does it bother you)?
- What if you just ignored it and let it go?
- What would you change if you could?
- Would it be important enough to change if you could?
- Would you be willing to sacrifice all the other good you get from the situation to change it?

I find that the using naked thinking, as we just did above, is often enough to begin the process of reducing the stressfulness of many situations. The very fact that at this point you realize it's really you that are stressing yourself out over these things and that you have a choice (and power) of what to do is like passing through a wall of smoke into a new land where things are far clearer and more controllable—like Dorothy stepping out of her black-and-white cabin into the colorful world of Oz. That sense of greater control is a source of strength and a means to managing the events with far less stress.

What about worry?

There are several types of stress we experience as a result of what our mind does with situations. For example, when a person says something to you, and you ruminate over it and go through every possible nuance of what it means, and then begins the litany of condemnations, you can work up quite a head of steam. Have you listened to those thoughts? They may sound something like these:

Worry

Continuously thinking about a negative outcome possibility as it relates to some real or imagined event—a type of obsessive thinking.

• Who does he think he is!
• What a jackass!
• She has no right to talk to me like that!
• I'll show him! I'll make his life as miserable as he's making mine!
• I can't believe she said that!
• I'll be darned if he thinks I'm ever going help him again!

Notice how I used exclamation points after each. The reason is simple: you aren't just talking to yourself about what happened; you're yelling at that person or the universe in your own head and carrying on a private inner dialogue with you. You can wind up far angrier over what you just said to yourself than you ever were or could justify over what that person said to you. (Have you ever said or heard, "The more I think about it, the madder I get!"?)

This kind of self-talk is what we'll call reliving. You relive events repeatedly, sometimes making things grow much worse from the internal dialogue. To reduce stress, feel less depression or anxiety, and be happier in general, you will want to stop this dialogue as soon as possible. Do not allow yourself one moment of reliving an interaction or event unless it's to analyze it for future benefit or to decide what to do when fixing it is required.

A distinct problem arises in the minds of many when faced with the idea of stopping yourself and not allowing yourself to continue to think about the way others have treated you or having experienced an event

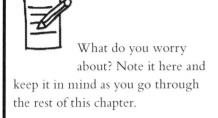

What do you worry about? Note it here and keep it in mind as you go through the rest of this chapter.

that had a negative outcome. People feel justified in being angry, hurt, resentful, and vengeful, so to not think about it seems like we are "letting them get away with it." Here is an example of what I mean and how it might look in the real world.

Miriam came to me as a patient for counseling because she found out her husband, Mark, had been cheating on her. She was forty-two and just had their fourth child about two months earlier. At one point, we had Mark in the office with us, and he looked her straight in the eye and told her the reason he did this was to prove to her that he could find someone else anytime and she'd better straighten up or he'd leave her. (Eek! Talk about an uncomfortable moment in the counselor's office!)

After several weeks of getting nowhere, I told Miriam I would have to stop seeing her because she wasn't ready to really let it go and get on with the marriage as she had agreed to a few weeks before. Mark had cut off all other relationships and had recommitted to their marriage, but she just couldn't do it. She relived every thought of the two of them together over and over every day. In fact, to make things more real, she parked her car and watched this "other woman" come out of her workplace to leave for home. Of course this woman was in her early twenties and gorgeous—at least according to Miriam.

This reliving was like watching a freight train with each boxcar billboarded with a scene from her husband's affair. One after another, it puffed and chugged through her mind, and every time it did, it was like it was happening all over again right now, today. It was becoming part of her to be depressed and aggrieved. It was becoming her identity, and Mark was sick of it. He said that he wasn't going to commit to a marriage that was nothing more than a life sentence of punishment from Miriam.

Without making judgments about Mark or Miriam, we were faced with a simple fact: unless Miriam was going to let this go and proceed with the relationship like this never happened, the relationship was over as far as Mark was concerned. I told her this, and she said to me, "So I just smile through this, and he gets everything he wants. He got his little affair, his wife and kids, and the freedom to do as he pleases, and all I get is to accept it and let it go. It just doesn't seem fair." And that last sentence said it all. To Miriam, and maybe to you, it doesn't seem fair, and so she had a hard time letting it go because her anger was justifiable. Perhaps it was, but the real question was whether she wanted to leave him, stay with him and let it go, or try to hang on and punish him and herself as long as he would allow.

Naked thinking allows us to see that something being justifiable doesn't make it a good thing to do. I was very sympathetic to Miriam, but I looked at her and told her directly that she would have to decide what she was going to do. She chose to let it go, and I helped her do that. After another four sessions, she terminated therapy and went on to find happiness with Mark and her children for many years. It wasn't easy for her, but it was necessary to stop reliving these events and just let them stop plowing through her mind regardless of whether it could be justified or not.

Worry is the exact same thing, but instead of reliving an event, you prelive an event. Instead of reliving the scenes of what has happened, you prelive all the various what-ifs that could or might happen. Over and over, like Miriam above, you see all the worst-case possibilities like billboards on the freight train plowing through your mind. The only way to stop this is to stop it. You must be willing to behave differently from the way you feel. Naked thinking is stripping away the guilt and shame of not thinking about it and then facing the worst-case outcome if it occurs.

Worry often starts out with what-ifs and ends with I-shouldas. You know what I mean. After something is finally done and it went badly, you start a new round of "I shoulda done this. I shoulda done that." And because you know you will do that to yourself, you prelive it because you will feel guilty for not having thought about it before it happened. Here's what I mean.

A doctor tells you your ten-year-old daughter may have the early signs of a kind of cancer. He tells you that there are tests they can do to be sure, and they will do them in about a week. You now have a perfect opportunity to prelive the worst thing that can ever happen to a parent—and you do. You go to the Internet and look up everything this cancer can cause and do to her. You cry your eyes out six times a day.

You tell everyone you know, and each and every one tells you not to worry, it'll all be okay. "But what if it's not!" you say. Well, if it's not, you will have an entirely different group of things you will have to consider and decide about. And if it's not okay, you will feel cold and heartless for having not worried! You will feel guilt and shame—guilt for being coldhearted and callous, and ashamed for having to admit to others that you didn't think about it quite so much.

And when the doctor comes back and tells you everything is fine just like he said it probably would be, you feel utter exhaustion. Why? Because this stressor has been used by your mind to prelive events that are exhausting. Your mind has had you on a metaphorical roller coaster, and the way you get off this roller coaster of worry is to start with naked thinking. Use naked thinking to strip down to the facts and leave the what-ifs alone until there is a decision to make. Refuse to feel guilt or shame for not feeling bad or anything else until there is something real to have feelings about. You must learn to do what Miriam did and let it go until there is something to actually do something about.

This seems to be a candidate for the old cliché, "that's easier said than done." Well, it is always easier to say something than it is to do something about the way we feel, or change a habit. Whether it's to lose weight, exercise more, or reduce the harmful effects of stress, talking about it is only a starting point. The rest is a matter of doing something that, over time, will change the habitual ways we handle what we handle now. Here is a step-by-step approach to do that. Notice that step number one means you must be willing to behave differently from the way you feel and step away from justifying the way you are now.

The Step-by-Step of Reducing Your Stress with Naked Thinking

1. **You must be committed to reducing stress and letting go of the fact that other people do things you don't like.** This is very hard for some of us. Many of us have been taught from the earliest parts of our lives to get upset with certain facial or hand gestures, tones of voice, concepts of fairness, and the like. The fact is, no matter what we do, other people will do what they do! We cannot make people stop doing everything we would prefer they not do. You must find a way to accept that and let it go. This is a matter of decision. You simply choose to do it or not. Remember that naked thinking is stripping away these unproductive or counterproductive emotions and doing what you know is best no matter how you feel.

2. **Use naked thinking to seriously evaluate what you stress yourself over.** If I were to ask you how much of your arm you'd be willing to lose in order to get someone to act like you want them to, you'd probably tell me none. When you begin to look at how overwrought you become over what others do and compare that to what you would be willing to do to yourself in order to make it stop (like a scale of just how awful is it really), you get a much more rational view of just how important this really is. Naked thinking—that is, without the suffocating effects of indignity, revenge, outrage, and a host of other strong emotions—would have you realize it is just another minor irritation, and that if you just ignored it, it would be relatively meaningless in your life.

3. **Use naked thinking to evaluate whether certain things are worth trying to change or better being completely dismissed.** Naked thinking isn't about learning how to be a doormat. It isn't in your best interest to just let everything go and "don't worry; be happy!" There are some things that you will deem important enough to do something about. Naked thinking allows you to judge that rationally and then approach a means of changing things with deliberateness and intentionality. This greatly increases your ability to think clearly, decide wisely, and do what you must more effectively.

4. **Use relaxation imagery to train yourself to feel less when these things do happen to you.** In psychology, we would call this a type

> **Use Naked Thinking to evaluate what to change and what to let go of.**
>
> A certain man drives to work on a congested road every day. Several time a day, someone will jump in front of him, cut him off, or do something else that seems like a bad idea on the road. He begins to scream at each one, going through his well-practiced litany of epithets. By the time he gets to work, he's a wreck. It keys him up so much he winds up with an emotional hair trigger for dealing with his coworkers.
>
> At night, he does it all again on his drive home. He plops down, has a couple of drinks, and essentially disappears in plain sight from his family.
>
> Here we have a prime example of how he cannot ever change the way others drive but can, with effort, let it go and stop eating himself up so there's nothing left for the people he loves or works with. This was an easy choice, though. Many are less clear, but naked thinking helps you make that judgment better—a judgment only you can make.

of desensitization. People use it to get over phobias. Find a comfortable place to lie back, close your eyes, and imagine this thing you don't like happening right now. As it does, take a deep breath and let it out slowly. As you do, feel yourself relax. Tell yourself to relax and let it go. When this happens in real life, take a surreptitious breath and breathe out slowly. Stay focused when you need to but also tell yourself to let it go and relax.

5. **Practice two or three times a day so you'll be ready when it happens in real life.** If you were going to throw a basketball into a hoop for a million dollars, you wouldn't wait until you were on the court to throw your first ball. You'd practice at home or the gym so when a throng of people are watching you, you can still make the throw. The same principle applies here. Practice several times a day and for an extra-long time when you reacted poorly to the same event. What I mean is, if you got upset when a coworker rolled his eyes at you today, today take an extra several minutes practicing letting it go when someone does that. You must practice in the real world and bring the real world into your practice.

In Conclusion

When we use the word *stress*, what we really mean is the bad feelings we get when we face the many struggles life is sure to challenge us with. Remember that stress is any outside force on our system. It isn't just the stuff we don't like. It also includes the pressure we feel in a contest or that tumbling feeling we get while waiting to see where the golf ball is going to land. It's the thrilling fear of a roller coaster or the wonder of whether it's a boy or a girl. Stress is all that as well as the emotional upheaval that eats at our gut sometimes. So, stress itself isn't bad, but when we get caught up with the multitude of certain events, it can have a devastating effect on both our minds and our bodies.

Naked thinking gives us a means to deal with these struggles in a different way. With naked thinking, we can see what happens in a clearer, more manageable way, giving us a better method to meet the issue and fret far less over the struggle itself. Once you master these simple steps (and continue to practice them), you can reduce the negative effects of stress and learn to live a more stress-free life.

The Naked-Thinking
Bully Barrier

Framework

What we call bullying has changed considerably over the years. Not long ago, bullying was a term used almost exclusively to refer to someone who uses some kind of power (or supposed power) to coerce someone to do something he or she doesn't want to do. We've all seen the cliché of the kid walking to school and being stopped by the neighborhood bully to make him cough up his lunch money. We are well past that today.

What is falling under the concept of bullying is almost anything that is considered unwanted behavior by someone. A bystander witnessing something that he or she doesn't want to see or hear may consider their having to see or hear it a form of bullying. Even unwanted compliments are considered bullying by some.

With such a wide-reaching and diffuse definition, it becomes very difficult for people with a duty to protect, such as school principals and the like, to know what to do. As a result, many do nothing while others adopt automatic, so-called zero-tolerance policies. The first approach can lead to subjecting some to significant and preventable mistreatment. The latter approach can lead to absurd overreactions that make matters worse and trivialize the real consequences of such behavior.

There are many issues that arise when considering what to do when a complaint of bullying arises. The first, of course, is to judge if what is being called bullying is indeed bullying and not some other kind of obnoxious behavior. In some environments, dealing with each slight and supposed insult could lead to a full-time job with an overly sensitive few in your universe. So there has to be some kind of working definition that leads to the efficient use of whatever remedies you would have.

Another element that must be addressed is whether this behavior is just obnoxious or if it's dangerous or even illegal. Here, too, we have the problem of personal judgments and biases pushing the solution toward what the authority figure uses as his or her default. For example, a school principal may fall on at-home suspension as his default means of handling certain behavior. Without realizing it, he may commonly and unconsciously define many incidents to fit this remedy. It isn't necessarily deliberate, but when you're busy and there is always the specter of a lawsuit or reprimand hanging in the air, we all tend to do what seems safe and easy.

For some reason, many fear the repercussions of calling the police and prosecuting what would be legitimately classified as criminal behavior, like stealing (as in the above mentioned lunch-money cliché), assault (threatening someone with immediate physical harm with or without a weapon), battery (actually having unwanted physical contact with another), or extortion (forcing action or obtaining something by illegal means through force or coercion). Bosses, principals, and others in some kind of positional authority are often reluctant to act within the system that is set up to address these activities and instead play the role of adjudicator and then the implementer of the penalty. When it's a child, parents often defer to the school and accept this as a suitable remedy.

But, as already stated, bullying now includes behaviors we cannot classify as criminal, and they are more than merely obnoxious. They can be a form of emotional warfare waged by a person or group against another (or others) for any number of reasons. Arrogance, jealousy, bigotry, and a host of other emotions-driven reasons may be at the core of the motivation to do this. Frankly, the reason why is of little importance when a remedy is sought for making it stop. When children are forced by law to be somewhere every day (as they must attend school), there is a duty to protect regardless of the motives. This then places us back to the previously mentioned starting point.

Basic Underpinning

It is impossible to prevent all activity that others do not like or is genuinely harmful. Changing the nature of everyone is not possible either, although over time a great number of changes can be fostered. For example, in the 1950s, it was expected for teenagers to smoke, this being especially true for males. To not smoke at that time was to be "not cool" (or hip or boss or to be square). Today, after many years of exposing the culture to the dangers of smoking (along with other cultural manipulations), it has become more acceptable to not smoke than to smoke cigarettes. Current trends in Hollywood seem to be reinvigorating the propensity to smoke. All of this shows that influence can be mustered, but you cannot ultimately change anything completely, even through laws of prohibition.

So, what can be done? The answer always begins with what outcome you want to accomplish. If, as we've alluded to in the previous paragraph, the outcome is to eliminate all bad behaviors, there is nothing that can be done. If we want the outcome to decrease the number of thefts, assaults, and extortions, we would look to find a way to motivate such would-be offenders to choose to not commit these acts. Of course, that would mean finding a way to make the price of doing these things much greater than not doing them, and the gains of not doing them far greater than doing them. The legal system is already fully set up to do just that.

If, on the other hand, we want to focus on our own children first and foremost, then there are many things we can do that do not involve anyone but our own family unit. Naked thinking is one of the most powerful elements you can employ to achieve that, but you must first become a naked thinker yourself or you will not be committed to moving forward with it.

What do I mean? The average person (and therefore, the average parent) often engages in what many psychologists refer to as making irrational demands on the universe. I call it "shoulding" on the universe. Whatever you call it, you must be willing to get past the fact that the world doesn't care what you think or how much you want something to change. It's going to be what it is, and the people in it will simply do what they are motivated to do. Where shoulding comes in is, when confronted with this truth, your mind immediately cuts in with "I shouldn't have to just accept that! People shouldn't do that! They should do the right thing (as I determine the right thing to be). People should X or shouldn't Y!"

While I agree that it would be nice if people did as your inner voice might say in protest, the world is as the world is (at least for now), and helping your child get along in it while being the happiest and most successful he or she can be isn't going to be served by if-only thinking. This is not problem solving. In fact, it's the opposite of problem solving because it fastens your feet to the floor and keeps you from moving forward into the realm of where things can at least be better. Again, you must be willing to let this go or you will not be able to use naked thinking yourself and so not be able to help your child develop his or her own naked-thinking bully barrier.

The Setup

We are talking about what I call a bully barrier, not bully prevention. The mind-sets brought to bear are completely different. For prevention, what you do focuses on the bully or prospective bully. Since targeting or profiling potential bullies would be unacceptable in most locations, you make generalizable, blanket rules of engagement, and then enforcement becomes almost a game of wits between perpetrator and protector. The game becomes almost absurd at times with protectors seeming supercilious and perpetrators almost wily. Such a game is a never-ending series of moves and countermoves. Little is accomplished, but all seem satisfied that at least some kind of effort is being made.

Workplaces and schools have to balance bully prevention with not targeting certain people or groups. It's a difficult balance. So, what is common is for the authority in place to establish some kind of rule that seems to prevent the unwanted behavior.

A problem is that some people are so motivated to commit some kind of action against another, they find loopholes or technicalities as their work-around. When you combine that with automatic punishments, you have a scenario where it looks like a cat chasing its own tail.

While it's hard to tailor everything to the individual, especially when you have some watching every move you make to be certain you aren't targeting someone, adopting some kind of discretion seems to be a valid alternative. But where, when, and to what degree becomes part of the dilemma itself.

In the realm of the professional protector, such as principals and work managers, this may seem to be an acceptable means of maintaining a balance of all the disparate interests. When it's your child being targeted, it's not. You want more than that. You want your own loved one to be protected from such assaults. That is where the naked-thinking bully barrier comes in.

For prevention, we look at the bully side of things. For the barrier, we look at the bullied side of things; that is, we look at your child.

As a parent, you want your child to have a wonderful, successful experience in school or work (or anywhere, including a marriage or love relationship). You can't protect them from everything and everyone. What you can do is train them to be less affected by what happens, take measures to decrease the probability of their occurrence, and have the emotional strength to implement any remedies if they are necessary, as in unwanted physical contact or threat.

So, what prevents this from happening now? What stops your child from using the array of possible remedies already available to stop being bullied; or, what stops them from its having little or no effect on them when it does happen? The answer is simple: it's all in how you think.

While the answer can be put simply, the application can be difficult to figure out. We can begin by going back to the definition of what naked thinking is. Naked thinking is critically thinking without the wet blanket of your emotions stifling you. It's clearheaded thinking stripped of the emotional cloak of fuzzy logic or the pressures of being pushed (or bullied for that matter) by your own emotions. Let's take a look at how that happens.

First, let's look at why someone does not use the remedies available. What are those remedies? As I mentioned earlier, one is calling the police and prosecuting illegal behavior (like assaults or threats, or battery or any unwanted physical contact). When your child (or anyone) is accosted, threatened, or even manhandled by another student (or coworker for that matter), the "bully" has committed an illegal act. In the workplace, there are steps to take, and each one carries a consequence that must be evaluated. In the schools, going to an authority figure (like a counselor or the principal) is an obvious possibility.

Why not do these? As I say, in the workplace, there are consequences all around for this step. You must evaluate what makes the most sense to do the most good. Here, fear, anger, resentment, pride, hatred, and other strong emotions can play far too great a role in your decision-making process. Yes, sometimes the cost to you (or your child) might be high, but courage is the ability to stand up to your strong emotions and do what is best for you in the long run. If your emotions are pushing you around or controlling your thinking, you may do whatever makes the emotional response feel better and not what serves you best.

In a younger child that may still be in school, these emotions also play a considerable role, but there is the social stigma and the possibility of having to accept finger-pointing and teasing by others. He or she may be shunned by some. They may fear the loss of the relationship even though the relationship is toxic. Children are poor judges of what makes for a healthy or useful relationship. It's our job to help them know and train them to think about it when decisions of importance must be made (as in sneaking out of school with someone in the middle of the day). Children in our society of today are very sensitive to social alienation and public retaliation. This itself is a coercive force that keeps a child frozen and doing nothing when a great deal could be done.

Finally, what about the non-illegal, noncriminal activity that others employ to make another person's life miserable? You know what I mean. What about the name calling and the harassing commentaries or invectives thrown at them in order to elicit a negative emotional response like hurt feelings and a sense of ugly or worthlessness? Of course, in many situations, the course of action would be the same as that above. But things can quickly get messy and fruitless as we also get into the semantics of it with who said what first and so on. Some bullies are very adept at hiding their tracks, and adjudication becomes very difficult. This is where naked thinking is critically important.

The Barrier

In "The Perfect Principle," we explored how our minds work and how events outside ourselves trigger inner self-talk that elicits an emotional response. That emotion then changes the way we think and literally modifies our ability to make judgments and decisions. That is why it is so common for many to slap their foreheads an hour after what they did and said, and say "I should have said X," or, "You know what I should have done? I should have Y!" What this "shoulding" shows us is that you already knew these things at the time (you didn't just learn about them in the interim hour), yet you didn't think about them at the time. Why not? Because your emotions change the way you think. To be able to think clearly under emotional pressure is often called thinking on your feet, but it is really the ability to do naked thinking.

The bully barrier is essentially a form of systematic desensitization, allowing you to feel much less when these events happen and thereby also freeing you to think more rationally, powerfully, and without regret. What systematic desensitization refers to is a process that, over time, helps a person become less affected by what they experience. Let's take a phobic response as an example and work through it to fully understand what I mean.

Let's say you have a phobic fear of snakes—not a fear but an exaggerated, incapacitating fear. The very idea of stumbling across one keeps you vigilant just walking to your car. The idea of going for a walk in a park or the woods has you break out in a sweat. You have an adrenaline response with elevated heart rate and shallow breathing. Your

Crossover Motivation

It is the use of a motivation to do one thing to make yourself want to or be willing to do something else.

For example, you've been putting off going to a doctor for your cough because you hate going. However, next week you're giving a presentation to your management team and want to make a good impression. You use the motivation to not cough during your talk to make yourself go see your doctor.

To use a crossover motivation on purpose is called discipline.

mouth may even go so dry you can hardly speak. This is a phobia, not a fear. (Victims of bullies may experience this as well.) Many people are afraid of snakes but would merely stop and let one pass without incident if it crossed their path. A person with no fear may walk up to one and take a closer look—maybe even pick it up if it doesn't look like a poisonous variety. (If you had such a phobia, that last sentence would have you on the floor!)

Now, let's add that your spouse wants to go on a three-day hike on the Appalachian Trail. You are absolutely and adamantly opposed. She (or he) pleads with you to get help so that in a year you can make the trip. You agree. The process you will go through is called progressive desensitization. By and large and in the most general terms, here is what you would experience going through it.

In the very first meeting, you would discuss the rationale for bothering with this. In other words (like what has been said many times above), you would evaluate whether this is really something you need to overcome and why. (For example, if you are an urbanite that will never step into a park or the woods as long as you live, so what if you're afraid of snakes? Accept it and get on with your life.) In this case, you have a clear and articulable reason—to hike the Appalachian Trail—so we decide to move forward with the process.

This first step is critical because it helps us find the motivation to do it. When it gets scary, we need to have a reason for continuing. We must have a touchstone or pillar to fasten our tether to so we don't spin out of control and let our fears stop us. Once we have this reason clearly understood and articulated (even written down), we can go back to it. This, as I say, is a critical element of the process. Remember—in this example, you are phobic. Your fears are always just below the threshold of taking you over.

Now we move through steps of just talking about snakes, to looking at a picture on the table, to holding the picture, to being in the room with a real one, to holding one in your hand. Piece by piece, step by step, we move through the process of your getting more and more comfortable with a snake and even to the point of having personal contact with one. Why? Your mind might say, "I'm okay with being near one in the room in a cage, but in the woods, one might fall out of a tree on me or zip across the path across my feet!" and that undermines everything else you've done. Remember, also, that you are doing this so you can hike in the woods where snakes definitely live, and even if the probability of seeing one is almost zero—it isn't zero. You not only need to be prepared for that unlikely possibility; you need the ammunition to shut down your unreasonable fears that prevent you from doing what you really want to do—go on a three-day adventure with your honey-bunny.

By now, you will possibly already know where this leads us in creating a bully barrier. The same process of desensitizing can be used to make your child more comfortable being assertive (as in assertiveness and self-confidence training). Assertiveness here means the ability to assert yourself or stand up for yourself and do what needs to be done to protect or defend yourself as a person or in your position. A child that is phobic of social stigma or being ostracized will crumble inside and keep this sense of helplessness to him or herself rather than speak out and do what can be done. Children need to learn and fully appreciate that there are risks to doing something and *not* doing something.

Here I want to reiterate an important point. I do not think treating people badly is okay. I am not saying that no matter what others say or do, you can or should just get over it, get on with it (GOI-GOWI). There will be some that will never quite get the difference between accepting that some things will happen no matter what you do and sanctioning or approving of those things. I accept that Leon Trotsky went from town to town in Soviet Russia killing hundreds a day in what was called the Red Terror. It is a fact. I accept that he did it. I do not approve of it. So I can talk about it without emotion as a useful point of discussing history. The same must be true about bullying. I accept that we can never stop it from happening entirely, but I do not approve of it.

The Steps for Creating the Bully Barrier

What can you do as a parent to help your children deal better with anything we might call bullying? The easy answer is that we can use cognitive-behavioral principles to train (teach or condition) them to accept that some people will say things they don't like, do things they wish they wouldn't do, say mean and ugly things to them about themselves that might really be true and sting to hear, and it's okay. The world still spins on its axis, and the sun will come up tomorrow. Here are some things to do:

1. When others say nasty things to you or your child, employ step one in the progressive desensitization process and evaluate whether there is a real need to do anything at all or just let it go. Fully discuss why this is important. Review the value of not being affected by it. Ask them to tell you what they see as good reasons to not let what other people say to them, or call them, bother them. Remind them of the long-standing knowledge of what's important with old sayings like "sticks and stones can

break my bones, but words can never hurt me." Or "water off a duck's back." These and many others have been around for so long because they speak to a truth somehow forgotten in our culture. Your child needs to understand the value of this process and really believe in it and believe they can really do it and benefit from it. (See "The Final Step: Move Your Mountains" for more information regarding this important step.)

2. Teach them that if they are confronted with physical or verbal threats or unwanted contact, they have a duty to themselves to report it and be a witness against it. Along with that, they may be teased for being a snitch (or rat or tattle-tale or whatever the current pejorative is), and that's okay too. That doesn't mean that it's good or acceptable behavior; it means that they—that is, your children—aren't what others say they are, and this is a passing part of their lives, and they will be stronger for it. (See "To Stay Afloat" to reinforce this concept. Read this chapter to them and discuss it openly and fully.)

3. Discuss with them what ugly things people may say to them, or what names they might be taunted with and not like. Let them tell you what they might be. Set aside some time to sit with them and practice saying those names or saying those mean and ugly things to them and talk about what it means to hear it and guide them to understanding how unimportant such epithets really are; after all, they know better about themselves than that. You can make it like a game. Children tend to give the same importance to such things as they are taught by others. Parents are just one place they get this guidance, but it is an important one.

They need to get used to hearing things like this and challenging their inner voice with its irrational acceptance of it as truth and applying such importance to it even if it is true. The Perfect Principle is an important ingredient to this process. You must know it and believe it yourself, and then you must sell it to them with all the vigor and confidence you can muster. They must believe it. They will face the challenge of their own doubts and fears when confronted with such behavior, and they must be prepared before they need it.

4. Encourage them to come to you the first time anything happens—not necessarily that you will do anything but so you can discuss it and reinforce the concepts the two of you are discussing now. Remind them that you are there to be a sounding board and someone to bounce things off of, every bit as much as being there to help them and be a font of knowledge. Be open about your limits and that you aren't there to fix everything for them but to help them find the best way to fix things for themselves. This strengthens their ego and helps to strengthen their ability to stand up to the bullies out there and within.

5. Remind them of all the features of decision making, beginning with evaluating whether it's really necessary to do anything or just let it go, as in step one. Then, start with what outcome you'd want to see as a result, the exploration of alternative ways to make that happen, the evaluation of each alternative, and then finally deciding which to implement and the follow-through.

These lessons aren't just about being bullied by others either. They can be used to not be corrupted by peer groups; not be led astray from their morality or code of conduct; not be manipulated by demagogues, politicians, sales reps, coaches, or bosses that would seek to use them and throw them away; not be seduced by the lure of drugs, love, or lust. The fact is naked thinking is the single most powerful way of being the master of your own destiny. There will always be temptations to stray, and stray at times we all shall, but it's clearheaded, cold-blooded thinking about consequences and what tomorrow might bring that keeps us best on the path to success, however we might define it.

Reduce Embarrassment and Self-Criticism—A Special Use of the Bully Barrier

One of the more devastating ways your emotions can hurt you is with what we can call embarrassment. I say we can call it that because it can include several things like shame, excessive or unwarranted guilt, and being overly self-conscious about what we do or our performance of it. It shows itself in full attack mode after we do something we believe others deem bad. It's like having our very own bully inside our own heads.

Do any of these statements or phrases sound like you?

- When I make a mistake in front of people, I freeze and feel really bad.
- If I trip in front of others, I make a comment about the rug or pavement.
- If I whistle to myself and find someone heard me, I get red faced and stop.
- I apologize for everything like breathing too loudly or coughing (add almost everything).
- I ask for compliments, usually backward, as in "I didn't do X too badly," or "Was Y okay?"
- I won't do things I'm not really good at if someone might see it.
- I use the expression "my fault" or something similar a lot.
- If I make an error in speech, I will find a way to say it again correctly even if I have to force it.
- When something happens that I feel embarrassed about, I think about it all day.
- I will tell others about what silly mistake I made with someone else, secretly wanting them to say it's okay.
- I tell myself I am stupid, a failure, a joke, not good at anything, and perhaps a worthless piece of dust.
- I call myself names, out loud or in my head, like jerk, moron, dummy, wimp, fat, ugly, and so on.

Of course, most of us have experienced being embarrassed and a fleeting few moments of self-deprecation. In some ways, some might argue, it's normal and even healthy. Having a rational or realistic view of ourselves means we are going to find fault with ourselves at least sometimes. But how much is enough, and how much is too much? That is a question that has no specific or universally applicable answer. Some of us have a high tolerance for criticism, whether it's from ourselves or from others. Others of us have a very low threshold and find it difficult to accept that anyone would find anything about us less than perfect.

If there is no specific answer you can apply all the time (like three times a day or twice a month would be okay), how do we know when we might benefit from doing something about our level of embarrassability? A guide for psychologists for many issues is whether or not it causes you a problem. If you have a high tolerance for criticism, then it's not a problem. If you have a low tolerance and you are among critical people, it might suggest you'd benefit from raising your tolerance and reducing your embarrassability.

Use the same principles discussed above in this chapter and "The Perfect Principle" to desensitize yourself and raise your threshold for embarrassment. It really is just another application of the same process and principles. The more often you apply them, the more comfortable they will be and the more automatically they will help to improve your life.

In Conclusion

The best barrier to the words and certain actions of others is to be strong and know you're strong. The more confident you are about your own self-worth, the less important the opinions of others become. Confidence is born from a real and rational understanding of our own ability to handle what the world might dish out, whatever anyone might have to say about us. It isn't always easy to find. It may take work to build it within yourself, but once you do, your guiding spirit when confronted with any difficult situation might be well summed up like this:

I don't know how
And I don't know when,
But I do know that
I will get through this.

BUILD YOUR SELF-CONFIDENCE WITH NAKED THINKING

Over more than a dozen years, I asked thousands of clients and audience members to tell me the traits, characteristics, and behaviors of those they would consider to be good or even great leaders. The top answers were usually one of five recurring favorites, but there was one that was almost always at or near number one. That is, the person most likely to become a leader at a critical time or phase of an event or project was one that would be willing to stand up and say, "Follow me!" That special something in us that allows us to stand up and say, "Follow me," is self-confidence.

Self-confidence is a psychological characteristic we all possess to some degree, and to different degrees in different situations. If we didn't have some level of self-confidence, we'd be so afraid to act we would never get behind the wheel of a car, pick up our children, or present ourselves to the public for work or enjoyment. It is a critical piece of our psychology, and without it we wouldn't survive.

Write down any thoughts as you read this material. Whether they're coherent or rambling, don't lose them.

For many of us, our self-confidence is not like a big bunch of grapes ready and waiting for the picking. It's more like withering raisins hanging on by the tiniest of threads. But the good news is we can do some very specific things to reinvigorate and build our self-confidence, giving us a far better chance to move ahead in our work life, love relationships, and a host of other very positive avenues.

To best find a way to develop our self-confidence, let's begin with understanding it and its foundational roots in our psychology. When we speak of self-confidence, we are talking about your belief in your own ability to do certain things like overcoming obstacles or meeting challenges in general. This belief is built on a couple of underlying elements: self-efficacy and self-image.

The term self-efficacy is one we rarely hear in everyday conversation, but it is fundamental to our ability to take on anything new or difficult. It means that we believe that we can accomplish what we set out to do. We often experience it as the unconscious first reaction to a problem. For example, let's say someone asks you if you'd be willing to do them a favor involving running an event, and you don't have a clue what it would entail. If your first response is, "Okay. Just tell me what you need me to do," the chances are you have a pretty good sense of self-efficacy. That is, even though you don't know what you might need to do, you believe you will be able to handle it whatever it is. If, on the other hand, your immediate response is more like, "Uh ... I don't know anything about event management. Maybe you'd better find someone else," this suggests you believe that you would not be able to meet that challenge and have a lesser degree of self-efficacy. (See the chapter "The Perfect Principle" for more details about self-efficacy.)

The second element is your self-image or sense of self-esteem. Do you see yourself as one who belongs in your own world? Do you see yourself as a fraud or a winner? Do you believe you're as good or worthy of respect and being heard as the person you're talking to? The answers you give to yourself would be an indication of your self-image and how well you esteem yourself. If the answers are negative, you will be far less likely to assert yourself.

Self-confidence comes from the Latin *fidere*, which means to trust, so self-confidence literally means to trust yourself. You build this sense of trust in yourself the same way you would build it in others. That is, you give people the opportunity to do something, observe how they handle it, and then decide that this behavior justifies giving them your trust. Most of us never think about where trust comes from or how to build it up, but somehow we do it. (See the chapter "Trust Is Never Earned" for details.)

A reason some of us lack this sense of trust is that we diminish our achievements or we forget to remember them. What naked thinking does is to help you put aside your negative thinking about yourself and make a realistic assessment of your abilities. Once you do that, you can begin the same process outlined above—namely to give yourself the opportunity to do something, observe how you handle it, and then decide that this behavior justifies giving you your trust.

The Step-by-Step of Building Your Self-Confidence

1. **You must convince yourself that building your self-confidence is worth your efforts**. Building your self-confidence may well take some time, so you must be committed to the process. In fact, you must be committed enough to keep going with it when you really don't want to anymore! Here are some things you can do to help create your commitment:

   - Write down all the things you could do more or better if you had the self-confidence to do it. These will be your motivators.
   - Create a list of times you didn't get or do what you wanted because you didn't have the confidence you needed to assert yourself.
   - Write down some of the things you want to accomplish when you've achieved a greater degree of self-confidence on

Write your lists here.

note cards. Place them around your environment at home or work as reminders to yourself that you are committed to building your sense of self. Use code if you worry about privacy.

- Tell what you're doing to someone you respect and trust that will be on your side to encourage you and keep you on track. Give them permission and even encourage them to ask you how you're doing. You will want to not disappoint them, and this will be another motivator as well as a source of strength to recommit when things aren't going as you might like.

You must be focused and committed, or this isn't a process for building your self-confidence. It will be another example for your mind to paint you as a failure. Remember that naked thinking is thinking stripped of the suffocating and oppressive nature of your strong emotions. You will want to be sure you don't feed those negative emotions to be even more oppressive by giving up easily or too early.

2. **Now note the many successes you already had in the past**. In a cognitive-behavioral approach, the point is to challenge your irrational or unfounded way of thinking and substitute a better, more realistic view of what you observe. Your previous conditioning or training (see "The Perfect Principle" for more detail) may have you diminishing those accomplishments in a way you never would if someone else did the same things.

A good way to generate your list is to find someone who loves you, cares about you, or at the very least knows you fairly well. You could say something like "I'm trying to create a reason for someone to trust me with an important undertaking, and I need to list out some of my accomplishments. Can you help me make a list? What might you put on my list of things I've done or can do well?" Naked thinking will require you to not slap each one down or dismiss them as irrelevant (this psychological distortion is called diminishing). You must accept that you are actually better at doing things than your own mind will allow you to believe.

3. **Use success imagery to relive those successes to increase your sense of pride and efficacy**. Close your eyes and visualize yourself doing some of the things on your list from step two. Do this two or three times a day for about three to five minutes. Don't fall asleep but be relaxed and really try to experience as many details in your image as you can, such as the temperature of the room, hearing the sounds around you, and so on. And make yourself feel the pride and happiness you would when you've done the job well, whatever it is.

4. **Create opportunities to push yourself into uncomfortable situations so you can practice your ability to meet new challenges**. Literally, find new ways to get past what some call the limit of your comfort zone. Look at the list you made in step one that outlines some of the times when you got or did less because you were not self-confident. Pick one and find another chance to do something like it. Don't expect it to go badly but remember it might. Even the most accomplished people still have times when things do not go their way. The real issue is how well you took it on and handled it, no matter what happened.

5. **Evaluate how you handled the challenge from step four and learn from it.** Analyze what you did and how well it went. If it went well, ask yourself why and note that each answer is another skill in your repertoire to be remembered and used again. If it didn't go well, use naked thinking to turn off the self-criticism and deprecation and just look for the factual elements that could be improved in the future. Then remember that this process of evaluation is itself a skill you can do and use as needed in the future.

6. **To use an old cliché, "Lather, rinse, repeat."** What I mean is do this many times and use the new successes as part of your

success imagery outlined in step three. Continue to look for new and find old successes to incorporate into your imagery. There is no reason to ever stop doing this. We all find ourselves in a quagmire of self-doubt at times, so these visualizations are helpful to everyone forever!

What can you do with your new greater sense of self-confidence? Here are just a few things:

- Assert yourself with your family members when it comes to obligations others put on you.
- Feel less guilty for saying no when you really want to just say no.
- Speak up at meetings at work or in a club setting or church. Let your ideas be heard.
- Manage your manager and be happier and more effective at work.
- Take up new hobbies, such as singing, playing an instrument, or art.
- Be a leader sometimes and not always a follower.
- Begin a health program like exercise or diet, believing it isn't a waste of time or that you'll fail.

The list is as long as your imagination. Be realistic. Be evaluative without being deprecating. Accept your "failures" as just something that happens and can give you insight into how to do things better in the future. Remember that naked thinking isn't about being robotic; it's about being rational and in touch with reality. It's about stepping out of your strong emotions so you can more clearly see the paths ahead of you and do a better job of choosing which road you'll take.

In Conclusion

Self-confidence isn't the same thing as braggadocio. It isn't arrogance or self-righteousness. It's the realistic belief in yourself and your abilities to do what's necessary when it's necessary to do something. Without it, you will be reluctant to take on new challenges. With it, you can put to use your very best you.

Goal Setting—The Quickest Path to Achievement

Framework

There are many ways to achieve success, but I think there are two main categories: intentionally and unintentionally. Understanding each and the positive and negative aspects of them will give us a platform to build a greater probability for achieving the success we may seek. I say "may seek" because there is a part of us that sometimes tells us we want something when we really don't want it. What we want is to want it or look like we want it to others.

One example of this is quitting smoking. Many smokers say they want to quit, but they really don't. They want to *want to quit* or they want others to think they want to quit because they are too embarrassed to say they like smoking and don't ever want to stop! So, before beginning any pursuit, make sure you know what it is you're really trying to do.

Some people are successful without even trying. They just go through life being who or what they are, and for some unknown reason, success seems to follow them and force itself upon them. I call these people unintentionally successful. (I also call them irritating as all get-out!) The good part of being unintentionally successful is that it requires no work. All you have to do is breathe and avoid doing something really horrible like running over a troop of Cub Scouts. Anything short of that seems to be excusable.

The bad part is that eventually, for most people, this seems to last for only a part of their lives. Often, it's that part of their life when building value in yourself is the most important thing you can do, such as when you're young, in school, beautiful, or athletically gifted. But because you find success and adulation without much effort, you ride your success wave and pay little attention to why you're successful and how to be successful when these reasons no longer exist. Then, one day, nothing seems to work anymore. Maybe you're not cute anymore. Maybe your gray hair and paunch doesn't get you as far as your charm did when you were younger.

Many things may be at work to make someone an unintentional success. One might be that they've learned to do one thing very well, and it is in very high demand. Such demand for most skills is short-lived. An example is some of the computer-based jobs that seemed to have had no limits for value or lifespan. The year 2000 proved to be a rude awakening for some that believed they could continue to write their own tickets forever. There is an old adage that says, "Before you can have, you must become." In other words, in order to have more money, you must become more valuable. To have more love, you must become more lovable and so on. So, you must constantly be on the quest of becoming whatever it is that will bring you what you want. In other words, you must constantly be willing to evolve or even reinvent yourself to be successful in your future.

The biggest drawback for being unintentionally successful is that when the success train runs out of steam, you don't know what to do to make it start up again—and you don't know what to look for to keep it from running out to begin with.

Being intentional means what it implies. That is, intentionally successful people have planned for success by doing certain things to deliberately create it and then monitoring their success along the way to make sure it happens. There are, of course, many ways to do that too. But what I've found as the surest way to get the best result is to use the process of creating and setting goals. Yes, it's certainly more of a bother than just getting up in the morning and allowing success to find you. And it can also mean that you can overanalyze and actually create a disaster. But it is also the best way to make certain that you are aware and in control so you can learn from what's happening and then be able to make shifts and changes as needed to avoid disaster and generate success. At the very least, if things go wrong, you have a mechanism in hand to help you understand why and become more proficient for the next pursuit.

Keeping that in mind, the next logical thing to do is to make your first goal learning everything you can about making and reaching goals. The following is a quick overview of the most important aspects of goal setting. Read it when you have a little extra time, and be sure to have a pen and notepad as you read.

How to Create and Reach Your Goals

Let's look at the qualities of goals and objectives for the purpose of understanding first what they are and what they can do for us in our pursuit of achievement. We will then look at how to create them in such a way as to permit us to use them as more than a guide. In fact, if we make our goals and objectives well, they become an impelling force that virtually pushes us to the next step along our path.

First, let's define it.

Goal

A goal is the measurable, tangible result of some activity, defined in advance so as to direct that activity to create that result. We will refer to that final result not as a goal but as our objective. All the activities necessary to achieve that objective are what we call our goals. If we were to map out what those activities or steps that we must take are, we would be looking at a list of goals that must be met in order to achieve that final objective. So, a goal is specific, tangible, and measurable.

Some reading this book may have read about goals and goal setting in other books, and so it's useful to be aware that there are semantic differences among those that write about goal setting. For our discussion, the fact that goals and objectives

Goal vs. Wish

Goal: By this time next year, I will have run a half marathon and will have qualified to run in the Boston Marathon. I will hang my number in this frame behind my desk.

Wish: I'm exercising more these days. I'd love to run in a marathon someday—maybe even the Boston Marathon!

The goal has specificity and a dated deadline with evidence of having reached it. The wish is a statement of want with nothing to define anything more than a dream.

are different and have different functions will become important.

Some, on the other hand, argue that the two, goals and objectives, are the same and therefore use them interchangeably. I see them as looking the same sometimes because the final goal is your objective but not always. For example, we may have as a goal to write a book. The reason, or what we hope to achieve by having it published and bought by consumers, might be to become wealthy. If we were suddenly to receive ten million dollars, we would have met our objective of becoming wealthy and may never reach our original goal of writing a book. In other words, for our discussion, the objective will be the overall final intended achievement, and goals are going to be the set of steps that must be executed to achieve that objective.

So, to begin to use our definitions of goals and objectives, we start with an objective, desire, or want that needs to be met for whatever reason. We then look at what would meet that need. Our ultimate goal then would be that measurable outcome that would give us that desired objective. The distinction is important because goals are meant as a means, not necessarily an end—a way to achieve some purpose, not the purpose itself. Here is an example that shows the difference and why it's important.

Let's say that you are lonely. You wish to not be lonely anymore. Not being lonely is your objective. Careful thought about what being lonely is and means to you leads you to conclude that having a certain number of friends or belonging to a certain number of groups might be a way of achieving your "not being lonely" anymore. So you might then make one of your goals in achieving this end to meet three new people within the next two weeks.

Go ahead and use this information to construct a goal right now. Refer back to it as you read on to see if you might improve it.

But what if these people you meet don't become your friends? Are you a failure? I would say no. After all, you met your goal of meeting those people. And even if you miss acquiring your ultimate objective of not being lonely, you have still been able to do what was required to be a success. Sometimes we notice that meeting our goals doesn't yield us our intended objective. Perhaps what this means isn't that we are failures but that we are setting the wrong goals for this particular outcome. This is a very valuable point to consider before abandoning your objective or putting a greater effort in continuing along your present course.

An important reason for making this distinction between attaining goals and objectives reflects on a key element of motivation; that is, you must believe you can do it. For example, since you met your goal of meeting three people in the two weeks, you have been a success. If you define your goal as your objective of not feeling lonely anymore, then you've failed. Once you see yourself as a failure, it can kill any motivation to continue to pursue your desired outcome; it undermines your belief in your ability to do this at all. If you can see the successful execution of each step as a success, even if it doesn't go as planned, you will continue to be motivated to move through all the necessary activities to meet your objective.

This is hard to do. At the risk of sounding like a cliché, each time a goal misses the mark, it becomes information that you can use to refocus your efforts toward becoming more effective. If we always knew exactly what we needed to do to get everything we wanted, we would always have everything we desired. It is a given that some goals will not yield the desired result along the way, and we must be willing to avoid seeing it as a failure and instead see it as a step in evaluating our plan.

Kinds of Goals

There are several kinds of goals.

- **General goals**: general goals are those that define our overall purpose for what we are doing. They might be our aim as stated in our mission statement. My general goal in business is stated in my mission statement: *it is my mission in life to help others improve theirs*. Overall, I am looking for ways to help other people change their lives in positive, meaningful ways. A method to help me do that might include presenting seminars. Another might be to get back into radio and do a program for personal development. And another might be to make myself affordably available to those who might need coaching. And all of these are to help me achieve my general goal of helping others.

• **Operative goals**. These are the goals most of us look at on a day-by-day, step-by-step basis. These operative goals can then be further distinguished as follows:

   ○ **Long-range** goals may be five years out, like a goal for employment after attending a specific trade or professional school. It could be something even further out like saving a certain amount of money by a specific date so you can start a family.

   ○ **Short-range** goals are usually those intermediary goals you achieve as milestones while on your way to reaching your long-range goal or objective. Indeed, some short-range goals can be so well defined that they give us a minute-by-minute, hour-by-hour plan for achieving a specific outcome.

The Benefits of Setting Goals

Goal setting helps people focus their intent on achieving a relevant, attainable piece of a larger whole that will give them the value they seek. If there is an objective, an overall aim for all activities, that seems quite worthy but questionably attainable, goals break the steps down into smaller, more manageable chunks that will build your belief and give a recurring source of positive reinforcement, which will maintain your motivation. (See chapter called "Life's a Selling Game.")

If you can achieve a piece of a six-month project today, you are a success today. You don't have to wait six months to experience that success. If you suffer a setback today, you can look forward to tomorrow for your next victory, not six months for that either. Rather than keeping an eye focused on something as intangible as an objective many months and sometimes years (as in education) away, you can maintain the power of motivation by taking it one step at a time and experiencing the achievement of each step as an end and not just a means.

Another benefit of setting goals is that of building a greater sense of self-efficacy. This can be defined as an inner sense of confidence in oneself, a belief that you can achieve something of value, even if it's difficult. This strengthening inner confidence gives one the ability and the desire to take on greater and greater challenges. The greater the challenge we overcome, or the more difficult the goal we achieve, the greater will be (or can be) our sense of self-efficacy.

We gain a sense of accomplishment, satisfaction, and self-esteem through the building of this psychological component. Goals give us a steady source of challenges. By using goal setting, we see our biggest efforts or problems broken down into workable chunks, and we are spared having to face what, in total, may seem to be insurmountable. This builds our beliefs in possibilities and builds our motivation.

There are some other benefits for setting goals as well. Goals clarify expectations. Sometimes, going through the process of setting goals can—for the first time—make it clear what it is you are supposed to do. Goals can relieve boredom. A goal for the day, the hour, or even the week can give an immediate purpose to what it is you are doing. It can increase the challenge and make for a more interesting set of thought processes than simply going through the motions yet again.

When goals are set and attained, and feedback is provided, you can increase your sense of satisfaction. This feedback can come from a supervisor, or it can come in the form of a compliment from a loved one who can share in the excitement or the celebration of your goal's attainment. It could be something more tangible than a compliment as well, such as a kiss, handshake, pat on the back, or a high five.

If you want to create a greater sense of team, or family, keep in mind the importance of giving feedback and recognition for others' goal achievement. This congratulation or adulation must be for real, and so those things you recognize in someone's achievement of must be somewhat difficult goals. If you praise an achievement that is too easy, you will not accomplish anything except to undermine your credibility and your perceived sincerity.

Cogito! Even the most complex achievement is the accumulation of simple tasks. Each may seem meaningless, but together they knit together the fabric of success. If it adds to the final success, no task is too unimportant to do. Break down large tasks into smaller units to create more opportunities for success.

Whose Goal Is It Anyway?

A song I used to sing when I was a boy made a very important point about human nature. The title says it all—"No Man Is an Island." While the song goes on to make a different point, here the idea is that our decisions are never completely free and clear of the influence of others. We live in communities of two (such as with your spouse or roommate, etc.) or many, many others, like those social butterflies that seem to be everywhere with everyone.

A secret about human psychology is that the pressure to conform to the image in the eyes of others is a major causal factor in what we do. I say causal because, especially for some, the influence of the opinions of others is so strong it will shape our thinking so that the decisions we make are insidiously affected, and therefore we don't even realize we are making them under such an influence.

When a psychologist discusses problems in your life with you, he (or she) is listening for the unsaid. He is watching your face and listening to your voice to determine, at least as best he can, how much of your problem you already know how to resolve, but you don't resolve it because the influences or concerns about the opinions of others are preventing you from accepting that resolution or stopping you from actually doing it. One of the reasons we may not be happy is that we know what we need to do but can't make ourselves do it. This is an important discovery because the entire focus of what to work on will shift from what to do to how to get past the stumbling blocks to doing it.

When you set an objective or mark out your goals, are they really yours? Are you certain that what you say you want to do is really what *you* want, or do you want to do something because your real goal is to be liked or accepted, such as when we say we want to quit smoking when we really don't. For some of us, we want others to like us, so our goal isn't to quit smoking; it is to look like we want to, to the right people, so we will be accepted or loved.

It cannot be overstressed that unless your goal is recognized for *what it really is*, you will go on to satisfy the others whose goal it really is while looking like a failure to yourself. If you don't really want to accomplish what you say you want, then all your efforts to please the other will be in vain because you will not be happy yourself—at least not when it comes to the big things.

For example, I've seen this many times in my psychology practice: a parent is a professional, a doctor, and her son or daughter is brought up to also become a doctor. Let's now say that that child wants very much to please the mother and struggles with all that is necessary to become a doctor. Let's also add that maybe he isn't all that bright when it comes to science or math, and he has a great love for the humanities or a knack for programming computers. He is quite accomplished in his off-time tinkering with a PC but is failing with his studies.

In his early twenties, he flunks out of med school. (Don't forget that image of looking like he wants to be a doctor.) Or, worse yet, he makes it through med school and becomes a doctor for a dozen years. He then begins to obsessively think about all those things he could have been, and his disappointment, depression, and resentment are directed on his spouse and kids. He may even blame his mother for pushing him or his father for not accepting him and protecting him from his mother. His resentment might keep him from having close, loving relationships. He may even quit or kill himself before he ever gets out of his forties.

Is this a far stretch? Not really. Fortunately, suicide is not the answer for most. I say fortunately because if you're not dead, there is always another chance to start over. But while most don't kill themselves, many think about it, and often these secret resentments and anger make the living very unsatisfying for both the person in question and all those in his life. The bottom is line is simple: make sure that your goals and objectives are really yours, even if some won't like them. If they aren't really yours, your heart will never really be in it.

Cogito! We all want to look good to others. But it is we and we alone that meet ourselves in that little room behind the eyeballs. And it is we alone that will make the final assessment that will leave us happy or craving approval. Check with him (your little "you" inside) first, last, and always.

Some Characteristics of Workable Goals

Too often, those who wish for us to accept their goal, such as a supervisor or parent, remain too involved in the process of what you are going to be doing rather than what you will be achieving. There really is an important distinction to be made between asking a person to "do" something and asking them to "accomplish" something. This difference is critical.

An example of asking someone to "do" something is telling them to have a report on your desk by three o'clock. At three, it is either there or not. But what is the intent behind having the report there? If it's so you can have it in triplicate for a meeting next week, then telling that person your reason may yield the exact same result (having the report finished and in print for the meeting), but when and where and how it happens may look different.

One of the reasons telling people what to do can be counterproductive is that the vision is lost and a psychological need to be in control of our own activities can get in the way of achieving the intended goal. Another reason why goals often aren't attained is that the person working to attain them wasn't at all, or only minimally, involved in creating them. Ideally, a good goal will have the fingerprints of the person who must work with them. If they do not, these goals will not be internalized, and/or they might become a source of resentment or an issue for a control conflict. This is referred to as having an internal locus of control.

Notice that this is a "feel" thing. Rationally, we may realize

Internal Locus of Control

Employee: I can't work with Jason. He came in here this morning and told me to A, B, and C!

Manager: Well, that is your job, and his is to tell you what to do.

Employee: Yeah! But he doesn't have to be so mean about it! He could have asked me instead of telling me like I work for him and not the XYZ Company.

As you can see, here we have a distinction without a difference except that the employee doesn't use Naked Thinking, and the feeling is a lack of personal control.

we are always really in control of what we do. But unconsciously, we must believe it because that gives us a sense, or feeling, that we are in control. Without this sense, the locus of control will become more of an issue than the goal itself.

So, a goal needs to be clearly defined beginning with the outcome, not the process. And the person who is to work with those goals must be involved in creating the steps necessary to achieve that outcome. By having him develop his own plan of action, there is buy-in, commitment, and accountability. Giving people accountability isn't about accusing them or punishing them if it doesn't work. What it does is eliminate a psychological backdoor that will permit them to fail to meet the goal and have it not be their fault since the goals were unreasonable and unreachable. After all, they didn't set them; you did, and you were wrong!

Another important characteristic for a goal is that it must be *directive*; that is, directed *toward* some specific end that is worthwhile to you. If you're unhappy, and your goal is to get *away from* something, you might achieve it without having accomplished your true goal, which might be to be happier than you were or would have been. In a sense, this kind of thinking can create a paradox. If what generates your activity is simply to avoid something in order to make yourself happier, you are thinking about what you don't want and not about what you really do want instead. If you set out to avoid or get away from something, where you wind up will be by chance and may echo the same problem you had to start with, and you're no better off.

An example can be seen in investing your money in stocks. In this example, we see a fellow that has finally put a few thousand dollars together in his savings account and decides to invest in some company so he can make his money grow. He reads a little and sees something about a small company with shares selling for very little money. He puts half his money into it, and within three months, the company fails, and he loses all his money. Dismayed as he is, he is not defeated. He is ready to invest what he has left.

At this point, his goal is to not lose again. This is a backward way of looking at things. You can avoid losing money by putting it in a safe and forgetting about it. This will limit his growth potential by looking not at the market for growth or gains but looking at a tiny piece of it that would help him avoid losses. If we were going to use our naked thinking approach and look for a more directive goal rather than one of avoidance, this fellow would clear his mind of the emotional flinch he got when he lost his investment. He would find a way to discharge that emotional energy and go through a more methodical means of looking for a company that might be solid enough to not fail yet energetic enough to increase its value over time. He might quell his embarrassment or pride and seek advice from someone that has been successful in doing this in the past. With this approach, the possibilities are endless.

The point is that a goal cannot be just to avoid, get away from, or be different if it is going to be truly effective for you. It needs to be one that moves you *toward* some specific outcome that you have carefully chosen.

Cogito! Every negative act is a positive act framed in a negative way. For example, to not have been eaten by a lion is to be alive and well. Always use positive, active terms when defining an outcome. To do a "not" is to simply not do.

The Characteristics of Good and Workable Goals

We have already touched on the trait that goals must have some limit in time or they are not really goals at all; they are desires or wishes. Let's explore this further since this particular characteristic is often forgotten.

Without a limit on time, there is no sense of urgency. Without a sense of urgency, there is really nothing to push you forward to anything at all. Time constraints feed a sense of urgency. As with a sporting event or a social event such as Thanksgiving or any of the holidays that incorporate rituals and customs, the closer you get to running out of time, the more frenzied is the activity to get things done. Creating such a deadline gives us a motivation for this frenzy of activity, so we do more.

Another aspect of this time quality is that there is a follow-up or feedback system in place to keep that sense of urgency. If you simply leave someone, including yourself, to their own devices, procrastination and forgetfulness will take their toll. We have so many things to remember that it becomes very important that there is some value, positive or negative, in remembering these goals.

A goal needs to be *specific*. One of the reasons so many people have trouble getting others to help them get what they want is that they themselves do not clearly see what they want. It is virtually impossible to get others to share your vision if you cannot see it yourself.

Another characteristic of a good goal is *obtrusiveness*. Once you make a goal, if you truly wish to achieve it, it needs to be so obtrusive that you cannot easily forget it or lay it aside. One way of making it obtrusive is to write it down. This helps you to clarify it in your own mind, but if you write it down, especially in several locations, you will continue to stumble across it as a continual reminder. Leave a three-by-five index card dangling from your rearview mirror. Tape one to your mirror in your bathroom. Place an oversized one on your calendar so it keeps sticking out. Write yourself notes about what you're trying to do and put them in your pocket or purse so you have to constantly come across them.

Make them *clear*. A goal must be understandable. There needs to be no room for ambiguity either in how it's written and understood by the writer or in how it will be read and understood by a reader. This means it must be written in precise terms and in detail, including time, people, outcome, and any limitations such as costs. Avoid the use of vague wording like *to know, to grasp the importance of, to appreciate,* or *to understand.* These vague words need to be avoided in measuring criteria for success as well. Use more

And excellent example of this kind of specificity is seen in a contract a lender has with a contractor to release money as the contractor finishes a construction project. Lenders will often say that they will release 25 percent of the funds when the building is 25 percent complete as defined by X. This "X" will be a complete list of what is accepted and/or not accepted as measuring what is meant by 25 percent. Penalties may also arise if this percentage isn't met within a certain time frame, as in: if builder fails to reach 25 percent completion by July 1, 2525, there will be a penalty of $200 per day for thirty days, and if still not reached, payment in full will be demanded.

Now the contractor has a clear goal of what and when to aim at.

exacting action words, such as *to write, complete, submit, identify, construct,* or *be.* The success criteria also need to be in specific terms, such as being identified with deadlines (by March 20), how often (twice a day by five o'clock), or by someone's approval (to the approval of …). This last one is not a good idea unless there is a clear criterion for approval and that person is just verifying that the criterion has been met.

Make them *operational.* To do you the most good, goals must be stated as some kind of action. Goals are do-things. They are stated to get something accomplished—the objective. So a goal is the measurable, achievable step or steps that must be completed to attain the objective. As such, they must be in the form of a verb imperative and include the criteria for success.

It is too easy when writing goals to get carried away. Once you get started, it seems the sky's the limit. This, of course, isn't true, so your goals need to be *realistic.* Another important characteristic is that a goal must be *reasonable.* That is, it must be achievable with reasonable effort. If the goal is too easy, there will be a lack of interest, resulting in boredom and procrastination. If it is too difficult, it will result in stress, and your lurking doubts will kill your motivation to try. Therefore, it must be a challenge, but it must also be realistically attainable, and seen to be so by all participants.

Finally, your goal must be *relevant.* Goals need to be relevant to each other and to all involved. If the participants can see no connection between and among the goals set, there will result a lack of interest. Again, there will be a lack of motivation, and what may begin is a system of distrust. Workers often begin to believe that the only reason why they are being asked to do certain things is to empower the boss. If there is no clear understanding of the relevancy of the goals, there is always room for suspicion.

For example, if a manager tells an employee to have a project completed, bound, and on her desk by two o'clock this Wednesday, we have an excellent goal (provided everyone agrees to the meaning of the term *completed*). If the employee knows that this project isn't due for two weeks, he may find himself focused on the purpose for this deadline, or the motive or hidden agenda for having it so early. A good manager would explain her reasons to get buy-in from the employee and make this goal theirs and not just her own.

Cogito! Only make your goals at your reach's boundaries if stretching your boundaries is your goal. Goals that work are achievable. Never set goals for others that are outside the realm of achievability, or you may kill their motivation to even try.

Five Steps to Get Others to Do What You Want

There are many ways to get others to cooperate with your requests. The easiest is to just ask someone to please do something. While it's the easiest, however, it isn't always the most effective. There are many people who will agree to do what you ask and then not do it.

In most cases, this annoying behavior is just that, annoying. But there are times when someone else's behavior is required for you to reach your goals. Sometimes, what they are currently doing needs to stop so you can move forward. In any case, getting others to act is often an important element for reaching your goals or the goals of a company if you are both employees.

There is a great myth that you cannot motivate others to act; you can only motivate yourself. The fact is you can only motivate others and not yourself. In order for you to motivate yourself, you must already be motivated to motivate yourself, so you are already motivated. If you were not motivated to motivate yourself, you wouldn't even try.

On the other hand, I can walk up to a complete stranger and ask him to stand on one foot and he might. His motivation might be to be nice to a stranger, to be silly, or it could even be to show off to a companion that he is a fun-loving kind of guy. If he says that he won't stand on one foot, I could offer to pay him a hundred dollars, hand the money to his companion for safekeeping, and tell him that the money is his if he'll do it. He might just do it for a hundred bucks. The point being, I motivated a complete stranger to do something they never even thought to do.

There are other things we can use as motivators or incentives. Rewards often work when dealing with people open to doing what you ask to begin with. Unfortunately, rewards are not as effective when dealing with someone who doesn't want to cooperate, and especially if he doesn't want to cooperate *with you*. Does that mean you can't get compliance? To be realistic, maybe you can't. After all, his greatest motivation might be to thwart you or cause you to fail at something. That's when you will want to use alternative motivators. (See "Discipline and Crossover Motivation" in section 2.)

Whatever you might do, if you are using naked thinking, you must be certain that it has been fully evaluated and worthy of what you do next. You need to do whatever you must in order to discharge whatever emotional response you get from the refusal and stay focused on your goals. Evaluate carefully, and maybe even ask someone else you trust for an evaluation. In naked thinking, we accept that our emotions can change the way we think, and so our judgment/evaluation may be clouded, and we might not know it.

An example of when you might want to use this method of getting compliance might be that you have a coworker that gives you the product of his work so you can then do your work-thing to it. You have deadlines for your work, and those deadlines get missed because your coworker doesn't get his work to you in time to meet them. You have discussed it with him numerous times, and he has agreed to do better numerous times but still doesn't. Now your manager is giving you grief and telling you you're going to have a bad performance review if it doesn't improve. She knows your problem, and she tells you to fix it. What now?

Here we have a clear case of someone else's behavior standing in the way of your reaching your goal of a good performance review and all that goes with it. You have reviewed your situation and believe it is important enough to do something about it. You have reviewed the possible outcomes if it doesn't and have decided that it's important enough, not to just do something but to do whatever it takes within the work realm to get it done.

Here are five steps in a method you can employ to get that cooperation, even if he or she doesn't want to give it to you, or means to but doesn't for whatever reason. Keep in mind the outcomes are not guaranteed, and you must understand that when you deal with other people. They have their methods and agendas. There will be new circumstances and consequences for you as you go through it. You must be continuously aware of your own emotional state and any looming fallout that might complicate things for you.

Use naked thinking to not get flustered and keep focused on the issue, not the person and not your emotions. It will be very easy to slide into a sense of anger, hatred, resentment, or any number of other emotional mind-sets that will motivate you to strike out and not be as effective. The method below can be used for anything that might arise between you and someone else. Remember to use naked thinking and stay focused.

The five steps to get what you want.

1. **Evaluate what you are asking for**. Is it really important? Is it worth what comes next? Is it worth taking it all the way to its conclusion if it involves implementing a consequence?

2. **Ask nicely**. Remember you are making a request. The other party always has a choice to refuse, and you'd rather they didn't. Don't get sucked into the mind-set that you shouldn't have to do this. You might hear, "Why should I have to be so nice? She isn't being nice! How come I have to be the one to give in? It's her job; she should be doing this anyway!" If you're hearing exclamation points in your head, you are not using naked thinking. Discharge your emotional response with some other activity and start there.

3. **Remind and emphasize**. Behavior change takes ongoing effort. Maybe there is no commitment. Maybe the other person means well, but this isn't their ordinary thing to do. Remind them that they agreed and you really need their help. If they continue to need reminding, emphasize that this is important to you and you must have compliance. Ask nicely again.

4. **Introduce a consequence**. Do not make an idle threat. This must be real and doable. You must be committed to move forward with this consequence, or you shouldn't introduce it. If you really

need compliance, you must really mean the consequence. This consequence could be to involve your manager, HR, a marriage counselor, leaving the relationship, suing, or whatever might make sense to do in your situation. But be aware of the effort, cost, and time before you introduce it.

5. **Implement the consequence**. This can be the hardest part of it all. We don't want to involve others like a manager or lawyers, so we become reluctant to actually follow through. The other person may be counting on that. If you introduce a consequence and don't follow through, you will be telling them that you aren't genuine. They will now be trained to believe they can do or treat you any way they want, and all you'll do is bluster and then give in. Again, to emphasize this point, if you introduce a consequence and then don't follow through with it, you will not just lose this issue; it will show anyone that sees it that you can be bullied or abused.

In Conclusion

Goal setting is the quickest way to focus your mind and attentions onto things you want to accomplish. It allows you to peel down a simple wish or desire into the elements necessary to actually have what that wish might be.

Another advantage is that it's a useful tool for evaluating whether what you think you want really is what you do want. Often, what we think we want is just the way to get to what we really are trying to achieve or obtain. The process of goal setting allows us to see the endgame, and once you do that, it opens you up to new ways of approaching it that may never have occurred to you. Naked thinking allows you to evaluate all possibilities without your emotions creating prejudgments and dismissing some of your best opportunities.

Summary of Section 1

In section 1, we explored the nature of emotions and the role they play in our lives. We found that they are important to making life worth living. Without our emotions, life would be free of the wonder and love that has us want to get up in the morning.

But we also found that emotions can stifle our ability to think clearly and see what becomes obvious hours later, once our emotions have diminished and our mind begins to clear. Emotions literally change the way we think, and making decisions about what we say or do while in the throes of a strong emotional event can leave us with significant consequences to face.

Changing the way we emotionally respond to our world helps us remain centered and focused so we are far more likely to make a decision to act that will stand the test of time. Making better decisions and acting with greater intentionality carries with it the additional benefit of leading us to live a life without regret. Regret isn't usually born of a decision gone badly. More often, it's born from a decision that was poorly made and can clearly be seen as such once the suffocating cloud of our emotions dissipates.

Section 1 gives us the underpinnings for stress reduction, greater self-confidence, and a host of new ways of dealing with people and events. By using these principles, we take greater control of our emotions, focus our thinking, and make better decisions with far fewer regrets.

The examples, exercises, and practices in section 1 help us to understand the principles and how they might look in real life. But life is complicated. Simple explanatory examples are useful only to a limited degree. It is common for a reader to then experience what might be called the "what abouts."

"What abouts" are questions that arise when an idea might be clear but its application is less so. As a result, in our own mind we begin to hear these questions as we move forward and try to use the new information in a world where we used to do other things so automatically. They sound like, "But what about when XXX?" These scenarios for application are as numerous as the events in your life. For many of us, that could be dozens a week. For others, dozens a day. Section 2 is all about those "what abouts."

SECTION 2

In section 1, we explored how to take on living with a more realistic and less emotions-driven approach, providing us with a greater chance for making better decisions and living a happier, more stress-free life. This approach is similar to that found in the principles of cognitive-behavioral therapy but applied to everyday living.

In section 2, we will focus on application. No strategy or method for doing anything is of value if you can't use it when you need to. It becomes little more than something interesting you read about and then forget. When that happens, we accomplish very little of what our main reason for starting at all was.

Section 2 is very different from section 1. In section 1, we talked about the principles directly so we might fully understand them. The exercises were meant to further that understanding. In section 2, I present stories, analogies, and fables to encourage you to apply what you've learned so far. At the end of each, the Cogito! is a quick wrap-up and a way to focus on the theme and point at hand. This is followed by real-life application in a relationship scenario (family, business, or any other) and then how to apply the concepts in your decision-making process.

With each story, you are challenged to stop and think through what you might do or how you might respond differently using the ideas and methods outlined in section 1. As you go through each chapter and before you see my explanation of how to apply what you've learned, make an effort to apply it on your own first, and then read on. You may even disagree with me and find a better or more personally useful application. That's okay because the real point is to give you a new way of seeing the situation, evaluating it, and then making a decision you can live with long after the emotion of the moment has passed.

The feel of section 2 is completely different. It is meant to be more like a series of short conversations you and I will have in order to lead you to a different way of thinking and feeling about many of life's events. Some may make you laugh. Others may have you crying. In any case, the point is to then take that story and use it as a grinding stone to sharpen your skill.

Let Us Hear from You

If you have questions or comments you would like to share, you can begin at www.NakedThinking.com/ResourceSectionII. You can also make comments on our Facebook page at Naked Thinking Book (https://www.facebook.com/Naked-Thinking-Book-418517308337334). If you wish to ask Phil D'Agostino a question directly or explore counseling, coaching, or training, e-mail him at Phil@NakedThinking.com.

ALFONSO'S DREAM

Recently, I visited Italy. Not to discover my roots (I am of Italian descent) but rather to visit a place that was so beautiful, my grandfather, Alfonso, never stopped talking about it, even a half century after he had left it. What was it about this place that was so terrific that he would never forget it? After coming home, I went through my memory banks and listened again—and more closely—to what I remembered him telling me. And suddenly it hit me. As beautiful a place as it is, the truly remarkable thing wasn't that he never stopped talking about it; it was that he never went back—ever—even for a visit.

At nineteen and with scarcely a dime in his pocket, he came through Ellis Island around the end of the first decade of the last century with little more than hope and the ability to cut hair. He worked hard and married a young girl from near his hometown. As a result, within a decade, he had gained a three-chair barbershop and three living children, and he had lost his newborn son while his wife wasted away in a hospital ward with tuberculosis. He let her die without suffering the pain of knowing her youngest had already gone on ahead of her.

Remember

The first principle of the cognitive behavioral approach is to stay in the present unless the past helps create a solution for the present.

Life was hard, yet life was good. He insisted that his children speak only English while he struggled with it the rest of his life. He earned a pretty good living and never gave up on himself or his children. And he told me to always do the right thing. Unfortunately, I lost his counsel before he could fully explain what he thought that was. But the lesson, I think, is still there to be heard.

Alfonso's dream was what we call the American Dream. That is, if you work hard and do the right thing, you can make it on your own. It was a dream of being self-reliant and personally responsible. It was a dream of being able to succeed on his own terms, because he was also able to fail on his own terms. It was a dream of independence and freedom to live the only life you get, to the fullest measure your talents can afford you.

My grandfather was never one for flag waving or preaching the ideals of Mom, apple pie, and the American way. Rather, he lived it and every day exemplified it in everything he did. But this is not a chapter dedicated to patriotism or American exceptionalism. His message to me wasn't about the good old USA. It was about simply doing what you do with a clean conscience and a good heart and taking responsibility for the outcome. It was about living—period.

Pop, as we used to call him, left us at age eighty-six when I was only fifteen. During those few precious years, he taught me that where you are or where you're from is not relevant. Neither is what you are or even what you were. What is important is what you will be and who will be in charge of making it so. Living is for living. It isn't an accidental occurrence in a great mystical plan. There is no need to focus on or worry about what comes next; whatever there may be after it's all over will still be there whenever that is. So to me, Alfonso's dream can be translated simply as this:

Work hard and be your own person. Don't be afraid to fail, because *without the ability to fail, there is no such thing as success.* Use your naked thinking to stay focused on what matters and how to bear up under setbacks. Live well and always do the right thing. And when that rap-rap-rap of the bare-boned knuckles on the hand of the man with a scythe comes knocking at your door … be very hard to find.

Cogito! Taking a new direction in your life can have great value and lead to great rewards. It can also be frightening, lonely, and fraught with setbacks and pitfalls. Naked thinking helps you to cut through the clutter of your emotions and focus on the headway you're really making and on your plans to keep you going. Life has no guarantees except that as long as you live, every day there will be a new hand dealt with new possibilities. Embrace it with confidence and don't let the fog of your emotions keep you from seeing progress.

Relationships: One of the great pitfalls in any relationship, whether personal or professional, is waiting for things to be better in the future. The fact is no relationship is perfect because even if it is right now, it won't stay that way—people change all the time, and so too, then, do relationships. Make a decision to either leave it or embrace it. If you decide to embrace it, understand that it is flawed, as all relationships will be. Find the best in it and focus on that while always looking for ways to sustain it or improve it. If this relationship is with your spouse, embracing it also means accepting that person as an individual that grapples with the same wonders about you as you do about them.

Do like Pop did in the story; stay in the present and don't be so concerned about how you got where your relationship is now. Instead, focus on where you want it to go and how to get there. Use naked thinking to set your own frustrations and fears aside and focus on what's wonderful in your life now, with him—with her. And also remember this: many never even get the chance to meet that special someone for life, even one that is flawed.

Decisions: There is always a right decision when faced with a problem to resolve. The real issue is knowing what it is. Usually, that is impossible until the decision is made, put into practice, and evaluated for results—all of which happen after the fact. We need to get over that and just do the best we can, celebrating when it works and learning from it when it doesn't.

What naked thinking helps us with is finding a way around the fear,

Decisions, Decisions!

Have you ever been driven crazy by someone who went to a doughnut or ice cream shop and just kept ticking off the various flavors? "Should I get a cream-filled? Maybe chocolate! Nah, maybe a fritter—yeah! That's what I want! No, wait." What do you do? What some do is to impatiently say, "Just pick one! It's a doughnut, not a wedding!"

But sometimes it is a wedding, or a job, or a college major, or a car—the point is, we can't know which is best until after it is decided and we see what happens.

Have criteria for making your decision. Write down the things this decision is supposed to do for you and then ask yourself if doing X will achieve it. But make how many things you consider or how long you take to decide part of the criteria. Then just do it. Learn from it later.

dread, or other strong emotions that interfere with our coming up with alternative ideas or implementing them. When the stakes are high, that means the consequences are great, and so will the reluctance to act or the impulse to act too quickly just to be done with it. Use your naked thinking to do neither by evaluating and using the process you developed in section 1.

As Alfonso's life shows us, it isn't about what decision we make nearly as much as simply making one and then accepting the outcome without condemnation or conceit. After all, we shall always have another day to mess another decision up or make another success. That's life.

Trust Is Never Earned

In recent months, several companies with which I've done consulting have asked me to address an issue they call trust. At first glance, you may think this is an easy thing to talk about. I assure you it isn't.

When CEOs, VPs, or managers talk about trust, they are very likely to have a different idea of what that is from the frontline employee. To management, it usually means that the rank and file believe what they are told and are willing to act on management's promise of rewards and good will. When you talk to the nonmanagement employee, trust often refers to not being set up, taken advantage of, or knifed in the back.

But the underlying concept of trust is the same. Whether we are talking about trusting your wife, husband, boss, employee, or anyone else, the idea of what trust is and where it comes from is a matter of decision. Here is my definition.

Trust: A decision people make to accept and/or believe what they may see, hear, or be told. Both trust and acceptance are states of being based on decision. And making a decision is a cognitive ("think") thing that comes from one simple but powerful human psychological element—motivation.

Since trust is a decision, and all decisions are based on a motivation, trust cannot be earned. At some point, a person simply decides to either give it or withhold it, whether consciously or unconsciously. Have you ever heard the question, "Why should (or would) I trust you?" This question is proof that there is an underlying decision to be made, and the questioner is looking for a reason to make the decision one way or the other.

Some believe that if you do certain things, trust will follow. I believe that trust may or could follow but doesn't always or necessarily. For example, you may have a long-standing relationship with someone. You never lie to that person, always offer the most intimate secrets of what you're thinking, and include her in every decision you make, yet she chooses to disbelieve (not trust) you. There are those that have been burned so many times in the past by others or have been conditioned to believe that people like you are not to be trusted, so no matter what you do, they just won't give you that trust.

This can be very frustrating to a person who is mindful of the responsibilities of trust and does everything in his or her power to deliver on promises. It can easily be the source of a break in a relationship. There have been many times in my counseling office where one party has pleaded with the other to be trusted, and the other just won't do it. After a while, a mind-set begins to develop that leads to a sense of futility. Then, possibly, since trust isn't even a potential reward for honor and integrity, the party begins to do whatever he or she chooses with no consideration for the other and begins to lead a secretive life.

It is important to realize two things when it comes to trust. One is that trust

Lisa is a division leader at a manufacturing firm. James was promoted to manager in her division and became one of her six direct reports. For three months, Lisa would give James directives for this group and then micromanage their implementation. This was discouraging for James and began to take its toll on his self-confidence, not to mention how annoying it was. James decided to confront the issue and discuss it with Lisa.

In the conversation, he expressed his appreciation for her watching out after him and his need to be trusted to carry out her directives with greater autonomy. He acknowledged that she didn't know him well but pointed out several instances over the last few months when she was uninvolved and he performed as expected and things went well. She agreed. He asked what else he might do in order for her to gain a greater confidence in him and give him greater latitude in carrying out his responsibilities. The entire interaction was professional and cordial in tone.

In the end, Lisa agreed to leave him alone and review his performance "after the fact" for the next three projects as a way of building her confidence in him and letting him strengthen his leadership role in the group. Within two months, James was on the same footing as the other five direct reports, and Lisa was then able to stay focused on her own initiatives.

is never earned. It is either given or not. The other is, if you don't give it to a person you're in a relationship with, then there really is no basis for more than a superficially functional association. At work, that may be fine. But in a marriage, friendship, or partnership, it almost assuredly means a dead end.

What to do? First, make sure you do what the other party says is necessary for him or her to trust you. That's right. If you don't know, ask them. And when you've done it—that is, when you've met that criteria—hold their feet to the fire and require that they give you the trust as promised. What may be holding them back is simple fear, and you must help them stand up to it and give you the chance to show them that you will be worthy of it. This experience gives them reason to continue to give you their trust in the future.

Never, ever breach a trust with someone important to you. (Of course, honorable people don't breach a trust even with those that are not important.) I don't know how you will ever know the real numbers, but I believe that there may be dozens of good experiences necessary to motivate someone to trust you. But for some, it takes only one bad experience for them to write you off forever and all times. It is better to experience the embarrassment of telling the truth than lie and get caught later. If this doesn't work for you, then just be honorable and never do anything you'll be ashamed of.

And finally, trust others. Be careful to whom you give this exceptional gift, but once you are in an intimate relationship of love, marriage, partnership, friendship, or some other similar rapport, make yourself trust. It can be frightening to put the fate or outcome of some important situation in the hands of others, but that is the nature of intimacy. If you don't do it, you remove one of the most important reasons for the other to trust you. This is an important result of moving through this process of using your naked thinking, taming your emotions, and focusing your thoughts.

Fear, an emotion, will stop you from giving trust to those that need it in order for them to be a real and intimate part of your life. If you go with the flow of your feel (or "go with your gut" as some may encourage you to do), you become a slave to your emotions and cripple your ability to move into a warm and rewarding relationship.

Keep in mind that giving trust to someone is a risk. It is always a risk. It is never not a risk. There is no one on the planet that might not use your trust against you. But the chance that your mom or dad, your wife or husband, and so on, will is probably much lower than a convicted con artist. At this point, some of you might be thinking, *Boy! You don't know my parents!* which goes to prove my point.

Part of your job is to use what you've learned about naked thinking and think through the evidence and risks and decide to whom it makes sense to give trust and from whom to withhold it. You may get it wrong whichever way you decide, but it will be for the right reasons, and you will be far better able to live with the outcome if you know you chose to trust someone based on what you thought was a good idea instead of what you were feeling at the time. Sure, trusting others opens you to being hurt. But if you are continuously protecting yourself, you will never really know the joy and value of what it means to be in love.

Cogito! If you want to be trusted, ask for it and then prove them right for having made the decision to give it to you. Trust never belongs to you. It is always a gift. Always treat it as one, and you'll receive it more often.

Relationships: There are several critical elements in creating a good, useful, ongoing relationship. One can be trust. I say "can be" and not "is" because there are many good relationships you can have where trust isn't even a consideration, such as a relationship you have with a cashier at a grocery store. You can argue that you do have trust in that you allow him to price your items correctly and then give you proper change or whatever, but this isn't trust in a given relationship; it's the kind of trust you have in general living in a civil society.

The kind of trust you might have in a real relationship will mean there is a measured risk. That means that if you give this person your trust and he or she fails in his or her use of it, there is a real and negative outcome or consequence for it. An example in the workplace might be that you hand off a part of a project to a coworker, trusting that she will have it finished on the agreed upon time so you can then move on with her input and not continuously monitor her progress.

It's that last part that requires trust. There are many in the workplace that just can't seem to let go and allow people to do their jobs for fear they won't do it correctly or on time. We call people like that control freaks, but it is really the manifestation of their fear to trust. The concept of naked thinking is to strip away the cloak of this smothering overlay of emotion and find the courage to just do it.

If you are a person who has a hard time letting go of that control and trusting others to do what they do, you have a few things you can try. The first is the scariest … just do it. That's correct. Just let go and let the chips fall where they may. Monitor yourself and your stress level for doing it. Notice if you sweat or begin drumming your fingers or bobbing your crossed legs as a nervous tick. These are signs that your unconscious mind is protesting and trying to get you to quit. This is common whenever you try to break any habit, and this is exactly what this is—a habit.

There are many things and many ways we behave habitually in a relationship that's ongoing. We develop them within it, and/or we drag it into the relationship from the past. In either case, a simple behavioral change can master it. Be aware of the aforementioned complaints by your unconscious mind though. Your unconscious mind doesn't like change and will tell you that different equals wrong! Bad! Maybe even evil! Like a baby who doesn't like to be put down, your inner voice may cry even louder for a while, but if left to cry itself out, it will grow more accustomed to it and accept it as the new norm.

If you still can't seem to desensitize yourself to the degree needed to give that trust, you may very well benefit from speaking to someone like a counselor to help you do it. Keeping the basic principles of a cognitive behavioral approach in mind, discovering why you don't trust people or that person is usually an unnecessary element for improving. Rather, what works most often is a means of dealing with the anxiety through a form of cognitive challenge to quell your irrational fear of allowing others to interact with you in this way.

In any event, in most ongoing or long-term relationships, it is almost always to your advantage to evaluate the need for and the benefits of giving trust and then find a way to do it. Remember that courage is the ability to stand up to any strong emotion and do what you think is the right thing to do anyway. Trust is a gift that often requires courage to give.

Decisions: The single most important need for trust in decision making is the need to trust yourself. If you define need, as I do, as any object, person, state of condition, or attitude required for a specific desired outcome to be created, achieved, or maintained, then you need to (or must) trust yourself, or you will never get past the thinking stage of decision making and into the actual implementation phase. As you see by the definition, your need is dependent on your wanted outcome of moving through the decision-making process and actually making the decision. Without giving yourself that trust to move forward, you won't move forward.

Many people fret for days or even months over a decision to do something. This paralysis is usually a result of fear of making a mistake. The fact is, if the decision is important, the bigger mistake may be to not make a decision. In some cases, it is better to go ahead and do something, monitor the results, and make adjustments as needed than it is to worry over the possibility it might not be perfect right out of the gate. In reality, few things really are.

The best use of this concept for decision making is to follow the principles outlined in the Relationships sections and improve the relationship you have with yourself. Remember that trust is a decision itself, based on a motivation to give it. You will increase your motivation to give yourself that trust as you increase your sense of self-efficacy and self-confidence by reminding yourself of the successes you've already had and not dwelling on your mistakes. Learn from them and then flush them from your sense of self.

You Don't Have Fear; You May Lack Confidence

One of the great things about living in North Carolina (as I do) is that it's in North Carolina. There is little more beautiful to me than the North Carolina wilderness.

Yesterday, I was alone on a trail new to me, near where I live. The trail wound for several miles through woods I didn't know existed. I walked for thirty minutes without even the hint of civilization and popped off the trail onto an old abandoned road. I decided to go left and see where it took me.

About fifty yards or so down the road, I looked back over my shoulder and realized, like a self-healing wound, the trail I came off of was gone. Here I was at least thirty minutes into the woods and not knowing which way to go to get back. I turned back to the road and kept walking as before and heard my inner voice say to me, "I'm sure you'll find your way out. Don't worry."

This is very much what happens in our lives every day in every imaginable situation. You come to a crossroads and have to decide to do something. You step forward into it, and unconsciously your mind tells you not to worry because you will be fine. But then there are times when we hear that little voice say, "You are in deep trouble. You just made a mistake. You are going to fail. What are you going to do now? Maybe you should just turn around and try to find your way back to where you started."

When your voice starts to talk to you like that, you feel the attendant emotion, fear, and can easily be driven by your emotions to do something that is less than helpful. This fear comes from not believing enough in your ability to create a success or handle a failure. But the underlying cause of your experience is a lack of confidence, not the presence of fear. Fear is simply your response to the absence of confidence, so if you want to experience fear less, be more confident.

"Wow, Phil. That's sounds great. How do you do that?"

I agree this sounds simplistic and just too easy to say be more confident. But you must first understand that *because you feel fear doesn't mean you have something to be afraid of.* If you don't buy that, you won't do what it takes to create a greater sense of confidence in yourself (See the chapter "The Perfect Principle" for a recap of self-efficacy.)

The way to create confidence is to review your successes and make yourself remember them each time you question your ability to do something. Never allow yourself to entertain the "Yabbits" that come into your life and feed on self-confidence. (To get the full picture, make your hand look like Little Bunny Foo-Foo with your index and middle fingers as rabbit ears. Then use your thumb like a big gaping mouth devouring everything in its way. That's what Yabbits do; they eat your dreams and cut away at your confidence.) You can hear them nibbling away with things like, "Yeah, but the last time … yeah, but what if … yeah, but this can really make you look bad if …" and on and on and on.

It isn't enough to be successful, though. You must make yourself aware of your success and remind yourself of that success when you are troubled most. When you are filled with the sense of self-confidence, there will be no room for fear. Keep this in mind that the fact that you are now reading this book means two things: (1) that I made it out of the woods to write it and (2) you have made it through every previous problem you've ever faced or you wouldn't be here to read it. You *can* face problems and beat them. How do I know? Because *you have* many, many times in the past.

Remember you are the master of your own emotional destiny. Don't let fear crowd out your self-confidence. With naked thinking and practice, you can become even more confident and more successful than maybe you even imagined. (See the chapter "Build Your Self-Confidence with Naked Thinking" for review.)

Cogito! Every time you try something new and different, it's going to feel strange, and there will always be the possibility that others will look at you and think things about you. You will need to get past that feeling of discomfort. If you let that stop you, you'll never do anything really new or important. And that is one of the greatest benefits of naked thinking.

Relationships: A client of mine told me that he was reluctant to enter into couple's counseling because he feared it would open up new reasons for him and his wife to fight. I told him he was right, it might.

But he said he really wanted the relationship to get better. He was just too afraid of what this might do. He was at a crossroads.

But improvement means different, and different requires you do something. You must be willing to move your foot off first base if you expect to get to second. Tethering yourself to the past keeps you neither in the past nor in the future. What it really does is suspend you, leaving you at the mercy of the vagaries of your situation. Decide whether this relationship is worth working on or not, and then actually do what your decision tells you.

Decisions: What makes a decision good isn't the outcome; it's the process of making it. Many good decisions don't give us the result we were hoping for. Some give us the opposite effect. In some ways, that is one of those things that

> **What is a good decision, and how do you make one?** The section on goal setting explores the concepts of good decision making, and each of the chapters in this section gives you insights and ideas of things that all lead to good decision making. But let's review a few things right here that may help.
>
> 1. A good decision is one that is carefully formulated with your outcome criteria in mind.
> 2. It is crafted when you are feeling little emotion and thinking clearly about outcomes and consequences.
> 3. It contains either time limits (by the end of today, I will …) or some other limits, like talking to three other people before deciding.
> 4. It is within your realm of realistically being accomplished. Saying you will have an MBA in two years while working full-time being a parent may be a worthy goal but likely unachievable.
> 5. It will be one you can live with even if things go badly. That means you ask yourself, "How will I respond if this doesn't work?" If you already know you can accept the result, it's a good decision.

make life interesting. (I know, some of you are already thinking, "I've had enough interesting. How about a little good?") Find a good way to mechanistically and repeatedly make good decisions and follow it. This will help to give you a confidence that will crowd out the fear of failing. Then remind yourself often that you do make good decisions, even if sometimes the outcomes are less than you'd like.

Balance and the Golden Mean

A certain man was in a hurry to get to an important meeting at work. As he was walking down the city sidewalk, he found a dollar bill on the path in front of him. He bent over, picked it up, and looked around to see who might have dropped it.

He called a fellow quickly walking away from the spot and asked him if he had lost it. The reply was a crisp "No." He then went into the shop next to where he found the money and asked the manager and each patron within if he or she had lost the dollar. Each in turn said "No."

Not wanting to keep what wasn't rightly his, he made his way up the street, stopping at each shop and asking each patron and employee, always getting the same response. After nearly an hour of trying his best to find the rightful owner, he went to the local police station and turned it in to the station chief and filled out all the forms required. He then left feeling good about himself for having done the right thing.

Arriving at work two and half hours late and having missed the very important meeting, he was fired. He went home and told his wife that he had been let go. When she asked why and he explained, she stood in disbelief for several seconds. She began to laugh uncontrollably for at least a minute, then cried the entire time she packed her bags as she left him for good.

The man was left without a job and without his wife, but in his mind, he had done the virtuous thing, and so he was justified for his actions. He soon died a lonely, penniless but justified man.

Some might think the moral of the story is that virtue is its own reward and that as long as you pursue virtue, as you believe it to be, nothing else matters. It isn't. The moral of this story is that anything, including pursuing a supposed virtue, can be destructive when it's made to be the entire focus of a person's life.

We don't live in a vacuum. Everything we do must work in concert with everything else in our lives. If we focus only on one thing, the others will suffer. If you focus solely on your family, your work will be diminished. If you focus solely on your work, your relationships will decay. Being out of balance is where your emotions of frustration, being overwhelmed, out of control, and anxious can come from. If you want to be in better control of your emotions, this is an excellent place to start.

The ancient Greeks held that the best way to be happy in life is to find a balance among all things that are important to you, calling it the golden mean. That is, not to pursue anything to such an extreme as to pursue it at the expense of something else important to you. The man in the story pursued his virtue of honesty at the cost of everything else. If it were a million dollars, such a hunt, at the right time, might make sense. But it was only a dollar. The idea of "Whether it's a dollar or a million dollars, it's all the same thing!" is just plain silly. The effort to find its owner was not in keeping with the value of what he found or his obligations to work and family.

I define balance in this way:

Balance: Keeping all aspects of a life in harmony—that is, to allot the amount of time, money, and emotional currency to each aspect of one's life that is consistent with the priority it holds.

Today, before you lay your head down on your pillow, review your life for just a minute or two. Are you keeping all the important aspects of your life in balance? Or are you just saying you are but in reality spending way too much time in one arena at the expense of another? Are you spending the time with your children, spouse, or other loved ones that is commensurate with their importance in your life? Are you spending enough time pursuing your goals and ambitions to be certain at some time in the future you don't harbor resentment against others for "holding you back""?

The truth is that you, and only you, spend your time. You, and only you, decide how to parcel it out. You, and only you, are the master of your own destiny. Are you shaping it as you want it to be? If not, then perhaps today is the day to stop and begin to rebalance, for as another ancient Greek saying ends, "for tomorrow you may die!"

Cogito! A key to a happy life is balance. We may have desires in many arenas, and each has its costs and its rewards. Balance isn't about sacrificing one thing over another; it's about whether, in the overall scheme of things in your life, it's worth the effort you're giving it.

Relationships: There is an old expression: "The customer is always right!" If you've ever had to deal with customers, you know just how wrong that statement is. But whether they are always right or not, the real question is, do you want to continue to have this person as a customer, keeping in mind that you, your family, and loved ones are your most important customers? Some customers (perhaps your spouse) are worth almost anything you'd have to do to keep and perhaps not. The point is that a balanced life (personal or business) comes from a conscious knowledge of the cost-benefit relationship of anything you do.

This may sound cold when talking about love or marriage, but whether it sounds cold or not, it is almost always true that at some point in any relationship, one or the other will wonder, *Is this really worth it?* This is an unconscious admission that

The point here is to balance the proportions of your analysis with the importance of the outcome of the decision. If you don't know where to have dinner, pare it down to two and flip a coin. If you're buying a new house or car, or deciding to move for a new job, be far more methodical. Gather information for and against each. Talk to others and have them try to persuade you to each. Listen to the negative naysayers to at least be sure you've thought through all the negative possibilities.

In a balanced life, big decisions require a big investment of your time and thinking—little ones, not so much.

even this intimate a relationship is always dependent on some kind of balance. Be aware and stay focused on this concept at least enough to know what you're doing and evaluate properly if it makes sense.

Decisions: In the management training classes I teach, we consider the concept of "tolerance." This doesn't refer to my being able to put up with your behavior or not. It is a measure of the deviation from perfect we can accept in a performance or outcome. For example, the tolerance for making a mistake in vascular surgery is zero, while that for painting the side of a barn is great. Balance means we consider what is reasonable for a tolerance in any decision we make.

Some are so concerned with making the absolutely most perfect decision that they are afraid to make any decision at all. A balanced life allows us to make lesser important decisions with little consideration and those with greater consequences with more. The key here is to consider this element of tolerance and then act in accordance with what you determine makes sense.

ARE YOU A BAG OF GRASS SEED?

While working in my backyard the other day, a grizzled old man in bib overalls pulled up in a beat-up old pickup truck (I think it used to be red). He removed his straw hat, wiped the tobacco stains from his creviced chin, and asked me for directions. After spending about two minutes giving him explicit information on how to get where he was going, he nodded toward my open garage.

"Mind if I ask you question?"

I said, "No, of course not."

"I noticed you're workin' out here in your yard, and there's a big ole bag of grass seed in there. What's it doin' in there?"

I told him I was saving it. He looked at me and said, "Mind if I give you a little advice?"

"No, please do."

Sal played guitar, but he wasn't very good because he had ever only played for fun. Some friends of his got him interested in bluegrass and encouraged him to learn how to flatpick, a difficult style requiring a great deal of effort.

After several months, he was invited to play with their group. Sal declined and never did play with them. He was not convinced he could ever be good enough to play with them, so he never really gave it the practice he needed. He still plays for fun but not flatpicking.

"No grass seed never did nobody no good sittin' in no bag. Whatcha waitin' for?"

"Well, I planted most of it and thought I'd use the rest if this doesn't do the trick."

"So, in other words, you think that plantin' the rest of it later if this don't work is better'n plantin' it now and bein' more sure it will? Like I said, no grass seed never did nobody no good sittin' in no bag."

He then thanked me and drove off.

As you might imagine, I was quite perplexed. After all, it made so much sense to me to hold back my reserve and use it if needed. But then I thought, *Why did I plant what I did?* The answer is that it is the best time to plant grass, so keeping the rest is a little like holding back some opportunity until a less than optimal time. And if the seed that I did plant grows, then what will I do with what is left in the bag? Keep it … for what? For it to rot or become too old to germinate?

Then the wisdom of what that old man said to me struck me like touching wires while fixing a light with the power on. "Beware the cautious man."

If you think something is worth the effort, don't hold back. Either do it or don't. An investor once asked me if something we were talking about was under-funded or not. He said that it was silly to put $50,000 into something that might fail when putting up $60,000 would guarantee it won't. Having owned several businesses of my own, I understood the logic well, but I hadn't really seen how to apply it to life in general until this old man in a pickup truck.

Take a look at what you're doing in your work or in your home life. Are you holding back? Are you withholding the very best of what you are and can do for some date in the future that may be too late to do you as much good? Are you "under funding" your marriage, parenting, love relationships, work, and personal pursuits because you aren't convinced you'll succeed before trying?

Then think again. You may be sabotaging yourself by being too cautious, too self-protective, and hedging your own bets. If something isn't worth your full 100 percent effort, then it probably isn't worth any effort at all … not if it's an important matter in your life. Use your naked thinking skill and evaluate what you're doing. Make sure it's something you really want to do, and then do it, do it, do it until it's done—or don't. And keep in mind this wisdom of the ages: "Beware the cautious man. No grass seed never did nobody no good sittin' in no bag!"

Cogito! Check your fears at the door and lose the ticket. If you can't decide to give something all you've got, you're not finished deciding. It is fear that makes you hold back. That's feeling, not thinking. Use your naked thinking to cut through the fog of the emotions and move forward with courage.

Relationships: After six weeks of seeing a couple in my counseling office, I told the man that we weren't making any progress and he wasn't doing as he promised, so I would have to terminate the process unless something changed. He looked me square in the eye, with his wife sitting six feet to his right, and told me that if he did what he promised and cut back his hours at work and some other things, "I would have a lesser job, make less money, and still have the same lousy marriage I have now." We terminated.

Here is a man that was holding back. He wasn't convinced his efforts would yield the results he wanted, so he put in only enough effort to look like he was putting in any effort at all. He can then fail and say, "At least I tried." But he didn't try … not really.

Relationships are not like any other part of your life. You aren't dealing with your lawn or a job or what happens on the golf course. Every relationship involves at least one other person. That person has an ego, and every ego requires a variety of things from you in order to make that relationship worth having. If we don't feed it, it dies. The trick is to figure out what it needs and then provide it.

When you know what it needs but then don't provide it all and with enthusiasm, you have a weak, anemic, and dying relationship. If this is with a spouse or girl/boyfriend, you are on your path to termination. If it's with a customer, that customer is now a candidate for your competitor. If it's with your employer, you will be first on the list when downsizing becomes a necessity. For that reason if none other, it only makes sense to take inventory of what your relationship really needs to thrive and then provide it fully.

Decisions: There are many decisions we make that have virtually no real consequence to them. One might be the decision to eat at Subway instead of Jason's Deli. Decisions like these are made with little or no conscious thought about how the decision was made. We don't really need to throw our full weight to the wheel of problem solving, so we don't. That in itself is a smart decision. Life gives us enough to concern ourselves with.

There are other decisions, however, that have profound and long-term consequences. Giving the same short shrift to these decisions can cost dearly—too dearly in some cases. This is when you must give it your all. In decision making, that means you methodically look at the issues and go through all the steps to be certain you've done the diligence due its value and consequence. Naked thinking is required at times, to put aside the emotional pull to slough it off or give it the old slapdash. If you don't find a way to give it your all, that decision will indeed be a candidate for a decision you will someday regret.

DISCIPLINE AND CROSSOVER MOTIVATION

One of the hardest things a person can do is make himself do something he really doesn't want to do just because he knows it's good for him. Motivation is not only a good thing; it is absolutely necessary before anyone will act to do anything. Here is my definition:

Motivation: A set of psychological factors, having been met, creates an impulsion to act. An internal impelling of someone to want or be willing to do something.

That means if someone is doing something, they must be motivated. If they are not doing it, they must not be motivated to do it, or they are motivated more to do something else. That is a fact. And that fact means that you must be motivated to do something or you won't do it. But what about doing things you aren't motivated to do? Why do we do them?

The answer is what I call "crossover motivation." Again a definition:

Crossover Motivation: The use of a motivation to do one thing to make yourself want or be willing to do something else.

For example, you really want to date a particular person, so you ask them out to do something you don't like to do (such as bowling) because they do like to go. Here you are not motivated to go bowling, but you use your want to date this person as your cause to go anyway. To use a crossover motivation on purpose is called **discipline**.

Place some examples of your use of crossover motivation in this box.

We will look at discipline in a moment, but notice that what motivates the person to act isn't the want to go bowling. There is a crossover desire to do or have a greater good that is accomplished through going bowling. It is a powerful way to overcome an emotional response to something (such as disgust or annoyance) and stay focused on a more reliable approach to achieving your ultimate goals. This can easily be applied to both life in general and work.

Think about those mornings in school or college when you had an eight o'clock calculus class you really didn't want to attend. You were far more motivated to snuggle back up to your pillow and fugetaboutit! But in most cases, you went to class. Why? Because in the back of your mind, you heard a little voice say, "You've already missed three classes, and one more means you flunk the course. If you want a good job (or to get into med or law or graduate school, or don't want to hear your parents nag), you better get your anatomy out of bed and into class." That is what you were trying to accomplish—not going to calculus.

Of course the crossover motivation might have been that you wanted to do well and you knew that missing the class would not help you do it. This is still not a direct motivation to be there. If you thought it was simply a review of what you already knew and you had three free skip days left, my bet is you would have turned back over and sawed logs.

In our everyday lives and at work, we often find ourselves having to do things we really don't want (an emotional state) to do, so we look for a way to make ourselves do them. Use this crossover motivation on purpose. Think about what larger purpose you serve in doing this unpleasant task—how it will help you or someone else in the longer run, or hurt you or someone else if you don't do it. Here is my definition for discipline:

Discipline: The ability to take the motivation for one thing and focus on it as a motivation to do something you neither want nor would be otherwise willing to do.

An example is that you are so motivated to get into graduate school that you use that motivator to make yourself study for an algebra exam tonight. You neither want nor would be otherwise willing to read algebra, but you use this alternate motivation as your impeller.

It is sometimes the job of a manager, supervisor, mom, dad, friend, or counselor to remind others of the larger picture or the greater vision that can be used as a crossover motivator. We all sometimes lose sight of our longer-term goals as we focus on the immediate. If you consciously look for crossover motivations for yourself and help others see the benefits of doing useful but unpleasant things, there will be a great deal more accomplished in your life and in the lives of those you love. This is the essence of courage, to stand up to strong emotions (such as dislike, disgust, complacency, indifference, etc.) and make yourself do the right thing. Try it once today and prove it to yourself.

Cogito! You can't enjoy the Christmas lights if you don't put them up. None of us likes to do what we don't like to do, but we very often like the result of doing it. Use your naked thinking skill to tame your emotions to keep your eye on your objective and forget the struggle. Nothing of value comes without it.

Relationships: I can't count how many times I've found myself avoiding a conversation with someone I knew was going to go ballistic on me! How about you? If we are in any way alike, and I believe we are all very much alike in this respect, avoiding these conversations is part of your mental makeup. As strange as you may think this is coming from me, I think it can be very useful *to* avoid them. The trick is to know when it's best to avoid them and to use naked thinking to not believe they are all better off avoided!

Review the *Five Steps to Get Others to Do What You Want* in the chapter on goal setting. Remember that the first step is to evaluate whether this issue is something worth addressing at all. Many of these issues take care of and fix themselves if we just let them die a natural death, and there are some issues between people who stand in the way of a good relationship if left unattended.

Once you've identified an issue as one of those, you must now find the motivation to engage that person and be prepared for what comes next. This is not about how to have that conversation but how and where to find the motivation to have it at all. Think through the costs of doing something and not. (Note: these costs include time, money, and emotional currency.) Stay focused on whatever it is that is important enough to you that has you decide this is one of the issues that must be resolved and not allowed to die. Be careful not to allow the other person's emotional response to drag you into one of your own. Use naked thinking and try to consciously stand outside looking in, to remain as dispassionate as you can.

Notes

Decisions: In drawing up a list of alternatives to use within your decision-making process, we often dismiss potentially good ones because of a type of "emotional flinch" response. As above, use naked thinking—that is, thinking shorn free of the wet blanket of your emotions— to see these alternatives and evaluate them for their value in the process in as cold-blooded, unemotional a way as possible. Remember there will always be time to feel something after the decision is made.

One last thing—emotions are often a desired part of an outcome. When making an important decision that has profound and long-lasting consequences, do the process as devoid of emotions as you can but don't discount your emotions as a factor in deciding what a good outcome would be. If a decision is one you'll never carry out because you would find it too repugnant, it isn't a good decision. You must take your emotional response to having to implement it into account. This is also true of the other parties if others are involved. I'll give you an example.

I've seen movies where someone is somehow trapped, and their decision is to cut off a limb with a toothpick they still have dangling from their lips as a solution (maybe slightly exaggerated). Okay, that might work, but how far would you really get? Once you got down to it, your fear of pain or bleeding to death would likely stop you. If you're trapped and a grizzly bear is coming your way, it might make for a better solution than becoming a meal, but in the real world, it might be better to put that particular alternative on a back burner and continue to develop other alternatives as long as you can before using the toothpick.

In the case of having to cut off a limb, the concept of crossover motivation is essential. You will likely not want to cut off your hand with a toothpick, but if you focus on the escape of a worse fate, you might be able to make yourself do it.

Randall and the Golden Glove

It was Christmas afternoon, and twelve-year-old Randall was lounging on the sofa watching cartoons. Toys were scattered all over the floor as were the boxes in which they came. Under one of those boxes were two toys crushed to oblivion from being inadvertently stepped on. Randall simply shrugged them off and threw them out with the trash. His father said, "Do you have any idea how much time your mother and I spent picking those gifts out?" To which Randall responded, "Gee, I'm sorry! What do want *me* to do about it?"

In May, Randall asked his father for a baseball glove so he could play in a league over the summer. His father told him that if he wanted a baseball glove, he would be glad to drive him to a store and let him buy one … with his own money. Randall had no money, as he quickly spent his money within days, if not hours, of his receiving any. So he had to find jobs that would pay him enough to buy his glove. And, his father added, he wasn't going to be the source of his employment.

For three weeks, mowing yards and cleaning gardens and garages in the sweltering southern heat, he saved his money. He then asked his father to take him to the store, and there they found the perfect glove … but it was four dollars more than he had saved. His father patted him on the head and told him not to worry. "Another week of working, and you'll have what you need." Randall was aghast, but the following Saturday, the two returned to the store, and Randall, with his own money, bought not only the glove but a brand-new baseball as well.

That was in 1962. Randall still has that glove and the tattered remains of the baseball to this very day, while every gift he received that previous Christmas was gone before the following Valentine's Day. Why? Almost every adult reading this knows the answer is that Randall worked for the glove but didn't for the gifts, so he valued the glove more. That is, he placed greater value on something he achieved through his own labors than on something easily acquired with no labor at all.

But what seems obvious to us as adults when we look at Randall is almost completely missed when we apply it to ourselves. As adults, we want many things, and we sometimes want, if not expect, for them to somehow be given to us. In the workplace, we want yearly raises and praise. We want time off and leave time to tend to our vet appointments. But what do we insist we give back in return?

As employers, we want loyalty and blind acceptance of new policies. We want employees to trust us and give us the benefit of the doubt. But what, as employers, managers, and supervisors, do we insist on giving back to the relationship to gain that trust? These unfounded and unrealistic expectations become the source of fuzzy thinking and great emotional turmoil.

It's been said that the only value that a given object has is whatever anyone is willing to spend on it. This is no different when we are talking about the bonds we create in a relationship. Whether it is between friends, family members, or relationships in the work place, the only value it has is what each party is willing to devote to it. That means, if we want a greater value placed on our efforts, we must be willing to make efforts that are also of greater value. *If we wish to be held in high esteem, we must be willing to do things that are esteem-able.*

Thomas Paine wrote, "What we attain too cheap we esteem too little; it is dearness only that gives everything its value." As a typical adult, when you tie your shoe properly in the morning, you do not think to yourself, *Wow, I am really great! I tied my shoe!* The reason is simple. Although you did an excellent job tying your shoe, it took no real effort. By now, tying your shoes well is almost automatic. So, too, is how well you do your job.

When my daughter was about six years old, we were watching an accomplished pianist play a very complicated piece and conduct the orchestra at the same time. I sat in awe. She, on the other hand, simply enjoyed the music. I said, "Wow, he makes it look so easy," to which she responded, "Well, Dad, that's because to him, it is." Since that day, I've been very unimpressed by how well people do things and far more impressed with what effort it takes to do them well. It is the sweat equity required in an activity that makes it worthwhile.

So the next time you find yourself complaining about how hard something is to achieve, remember that if it were easy to achieve, it wouldn't be worth achieving it at all. Be glad that there is some struggle in your life, for it is the struggle that makes the things you achieve, like that achieved by Randall ... a golden glove.

Cogito! Go to the Internet, a bookstore, or a library and pick out something to read from a well-known philosopher and pick their arguments apart. Tell your family members that you're doing this exercise and allow them to question you about it until you are completely exasperated and unable to go any further. This exercise isn't about philosophy. It is about the ability to make your mind go places it's never been or maybe where you haven't taken it in too long a time. The brain is like a muscle—it needs exercise.

Relationships: I've been a marriage counselor for many years. One thing many find strange for me to say is that a good relationship shouldn't be so hard to make work. I believe it a fact that compatible people have a much easier time getting along with each other than incompatible people do. In the workplace or with customers, however, we have to deal with what we get ... or usually anyway. Sometimes the way we can really solidify a relationship is to tackle a really hard issue and work it through together. Like Randall above, we will find the relationship far more valuable when the struggle is over. This extra-tough stuff we just did is like tempering steel. The process is hell hot, but the results are often something much stronger than before.

Decisions: Making a good decision means doing your due diligence. The diligence that is due of course depends on the significance of the impact of its consequences. When the stakes are high, the diligence due will also be high and require a great deal of effort. Things like researching alternatives, evaluating alternatives, getting feedback or input from other stakeholders, if any, selling them on the alternative you believe is best, and then doing what is necessary to appear to be standing by it when it unfolds. (Yes, I said *appearing to* because just doing so isn't enough; you have to be seen as doing so to gain buy-in and support for this and other decisions of the future.)

The more consequential, the greater the required effort and the greater the rewards for doing it right. Remember that a good decision is determined by the process and not necessarily by the outcome. Being able to revel in the success of a difficult decision is easy and requires very little effort after the fact. The ability to make a good decision and deal with a bad outcome will require that you did everything you could to make as certain as possible you did the right things. Anything less will leave you with regret. Like Randall's glove and as Thomas Paine reminds us, what is too cheaply gained doesn't have the same value as what we struggle to achieve. Do the hard stuff, and you will never regret any decision you make.

LIFE IS A "DO" THING

It was a dismal Tuesday around six thirty in the evening, and Judy was sitting in my psychology office instead of being somewhere out there having a good time. Wringing a tear-soaked tissue, she was asking me how to meet a man that she could love and make a life with. She wanted someone who wasn't a "cigarette-smoking, beer-drinking, girl-slapping" creep, which evidently described her previous boyfriends. "I'm thirty-two years old," she sobbed, "and I can't seem to find the right Mr. Right."

As her therapist, it was my job to do more than just empathetically shake my head and ask, "How does that make you feel?" After all, she had just told me she felt awful. She wanted me to help her find something that was important to her, so I asked her where she had been looking up till now. You can already guess her reply—in bars! "And," she added, "nowadays, no one even comes up to talk to me."

This is when a little (actually very big) light went off in my head. She'd been looking in the wrong place, and she wasn't really looking at all—she was waiting to be found by what she wanted. This is an inefficient way to find success—that is, to plant yourself in the wrong place and wait for success to find you.

Based on my decades of experience as a therapist, I've found the two biggest reasons people find so little of the success they crave is that they either don't know what to do to be successful or they do know but then don't do it. If you give it just a nanosecond of thought, you can see that the first reason is really part of the second. That is, if you don't know what to do to achieve your goals, then you need to *go find out*—life, and finding desired success, is a do thing. Thinking about it or feeling bad about it isn't going to do it for you.

We hear stories of people who were discovered and became overnight successes. We see people in movies or hear people on CDs that seem to have absolutely no talent at all, yet they make gazillions of dollars and accrue wild success and fame. We often think that we, too, *can do that*, but we don't. And therein lies the problem: *we don't do that* or anything else.

Almost two thousand years ago, Jesus said the following:

Knock and it will be opened.
Ask and it will be answered.
Seek and you will find.

I shall leave any religious interpretations to others; rather, let's look at the deep understanding of human nature expressed in these three short exhortations. Notice that opportunities being opened to you, answers being revealed, and the mysteries of wonders exposed are all achievable after some action on your part. If you want a door of opportunity to be opened to you, you must knock on it. If you desire to know a truth or someone's heart, you must ask for it. If you wish to find that which will fill your heart with joy and completion, you must seek it out. You can't just plant yourself in the wrong place and expect it to find you.

Do you want to be happier and more successful? Do you really want to improve your relationships and make better decisions? There are some that may answer no, and that's all right; not everyone is dissatisfied with their current state of being. But if you are one that believes you're in a rut, perhaps even losing ground, or just waiting for things to "settle down," here are some actions to take that may get you back on track:

1. Ask yourself what defines success. When Judy first began to lay out her problem to me, she didn't tell me what success meant for her. What she told me was what failure was and that she was trying to avoid more of it. Start with looking for a clear definition with measurable criteria for success in whatever you desire.

2. Check your current status in relation to your criteria. Are you already moving toward that goal in some way, or are you starting from zero? Are you equipped with the knowledge to move forward or do you need to find out more and perhaps seek the counsel of someone else?

3. After reviewing your answers to the two first questions, what do you need and where do you need to be in order to find or

create these criteria? Think about it. How can you be a successful movie actor if you're looking in Kiwi, West Virginia? Do they even make big-time movies there?

4. Create a plan of action. Make sure you map out what you want to do with time lines and specifics. For example, "By next Saturday, I will talk to three new people about doing something together."

5. Finally, you must knock, ask, and seek; or, you must then actually execute your plan. After all, life is a do thing. Otherwise, yours is not a plan; it is a wish, and *in the real world, wishes do not come true.* One must do something to make a wish become a reality.

> **What did Judy do?** After several sessions with me and realizing that her problem finding a good fit as a mate might not be that she is just an awful person, she decided to change her approach. She joined two Meetup groups that fit her interests. This not only introduced her to others that shared her interests, the groups were interesting in their own right.
>
> She began attending business socials and contact-exchange groups, as well as volunteering for a group at her church. All of these venues exposed her to a different group of people, and most of them were interested in the same kinds of things she was. After a couple of months, she began dating two guys, and two months later, she was engaged to one. I never met him, but she told me he was the one she was meant to meet, so the wait had been worth it.

After four months of trying something new, Judy found her "dream man." The last I heard, she was happy with the result. But what made that happen for her wasn't wishing it to be (that is just thinking about it or feeling some emotion for not having it already). It was seeking out what she didn't know, asking for help, and knocking on the doors of opportunity she found. Life isn't a waiting room for dreamers; it really is a *do* thing.

Cogito! All success begins with knowing what success is. Success isn't really attainable if it's just to avoid failure. If you start at that point, your only option is to do as little as possible so as to not mess it up. Always start with the question, "If I could wave a magic wand and have the exact outcome I want, what would it need to be (what does it have to "look like" in detail) in order for me to be truly happy with the result?" Once you know that, the rest is paperwork.

Relationships: It is common to speak with one member of a relationship and hear a deep and profound sense of hopelessness in their voice. When I do, I will ask, "So, what have you done so far to fix it?" The most common response is, "Nothing! He (or she) is going to have to want to fix it, and I'll be here when he does!" This response is fully enwrapped in emotions. There is very little thinking in it. But what is the genesis of this emotion? What is the root cause of this sense of resentment or entitlement? It might be very different from your first thoughts.

While I do not profess to know the hearts of others, I have come to believe that the most common reason for these particular emotions is a lack of knowing what to do about it. When you run out of ideas and can no longer think of anything else to do to fix a relationship, people will often default into a sense of "I've already done everything I can. The rest is up to him/her." If that's what you think, you're kind of done. It doesn't mean there *isn't* something else you can do, but it sure feels like it.

Keep in mind that life is a do thing. If you stay put, do a lot of feeling bad feelings (like anger, resentment, fear, depression, etc.), and wait for the world to fix this for you, you may very well wind up as Judy did before seeing me. At this point, the most useful thing to do is to reevaluate this relationship as discussed above. If the analysis is that this relationship is important to keep (e.g., an exceptional customer, a great workplace, a spouse, an offspring), then it's time to do something— almost anything would be better.

And by doing something, I mean for you to go about the job of seeking advice, knocking on the door of knowledge by looking things up on the Internet or in books, or asking someone for help—perhaps even that other special person with whom you're having the difficulty! Why not? Think about it. How likely would you be to put someone down if they came to you and said, "I seem to be making a lot of mistakes with you, and I really want to find a way to work things out. What can I do that might help?" This isn't the answer all the time, but it might just be the best alternative now. But whether it is or not, the real point here is that you're actively knocking, asking, and seeking. This is naked thinking in action. And if it doesn't work out, you'll not have regret because then you will know you actually did do everything you could. There is real value in that.

Decisions: As discussed above in the Relationships section, making decisions you'll never regret requires you do your due diligence. Note the term *do*. You don't just think about it a little and move on. Sometimes a short conversation with someone you trust is all that is required to step across that

And what can you do?

Go back through the steps above and note what you might do to improve an important relationship in your life.

great divide between a decision and a great decision you won't regret making. It could very easily be something as simple as, "Hey, I'm thinking about doing ABC. What do you think?" or, "Try to talk me out of it." This latter version opens the door to active criticism allowing you see if there are any downsides to your decision you may never have thought of.

The more you actively pursue information for alternatives and for evaluating those alternatives, the more likely you will make a good decision and the more likely it will be one you won't regret making no matter how it turns out. Life is a do thing, and so is decision making.

FINGONO'S TRAP

Once there were two men that stayed out all night under the stars contemplating the nature of the Sun. Suddenly, it dawned on them!

It's been said that there are three kinds of people:

- those that make things happen
- those that watch things happen
- those that stand in the way of things happening

I'd like to add a fourth: those that talk about things happening and then take credit if the things do happen and deflect fault if they don't.

Before you think my pen is aimed in your direction only (yes, it is in your direction as well), I will freely, though ashamedly, admit this also applies to me. The fact is we all talk a lot about what we *might* do, or could do, or what should be done and then do not participate in making it happen.

Go through your memory and think about how many people you've known that have talked and talked until your ears hurt and then never did any of if. Isn't it maddening? What's worse, it's unproductive and, in some cases, counterproductive.

Its being unproductive may seem self-evident, but allow me to point it out anyway. Some believe that every great act begins with a great thought (or dream), and then after being fleshed out (talked about), it becomes a goal you pursue and then an achievement you've accomplished. I agree that these are the steps to a great happening. But notice that the end of the statement includes action. In the case of the two contemplative men mentioned above, there was no action but to wait for something to happen to them.

This process is a lot like buying a Valentine's Day card or candy. Being honest with yourself, it's very easy and doesn't take a whole lot of sweat to order a gift online or yank a card off the rack as you make your way to the grocery checkout. Many parents and spouses make up for the time they don't spend with their loved ones by throwing money at the relationship in the form of gifts that take virtually no effort. (Like, "Here's my credit card. Go buy yourself a nice little something that makes me look good to you!")

In the workplace, this is very much the same. The talk-a-talk-a-talk makes it seem as though you are really trying to make things better—like you really care and are putting a lot of effort into trying to fix it. But the reality is that you are doing nothing more than throwing emotional currency at it—and in most cases someone else's because they're having to listen to you gripe about it!

But how can it be counterproductive? This one is a little sneakier. When some of us spend a lot of time talking about a condition—that is, a problem or a dream we would like to come true—we eventually come upon some plan that could work. The very knowledge that we could fix something sometimes gives us a sense of satisfaction that satiates our need to actually do it. This sense of self-satisfaction then stands in the way of your motivation to really make things happen. I call it "Fingono's Trap" from the Italian *fingere*, which means to pretend. What can we do to break free of Fingono's Trap?

There are two things we might want to accomplish. One is to stop ourselves, and the other is to stop others from getting trapped to start with. Stopping ourselves is easier in one sense and harder in another. It's easier in that we are in control of ourselves and can therefore make ourselves stop. But since we do it so much and so easily, it's difficult for us to even notice that we're doing it. Until we do notice, we don't or can't do anything about it. So whether it's for yourself or for stopping others, the first step is becoming aware.

Gloria, Frank, and Gene were discussing how much they like to camp out and hike. Gloria enthusiastically stated that it would great if they all went for a hike on the Appalachian Trail. Gene was gung-ho, and Frank was interested. "Let's do this!" said Gloria. "We can go at the end of May." "Sounds great," Gene said. Gloria then went on to talk about who else might want to go and all the places they might stop. She then told Gene, "You ought to get permits so we don't miss out on the use of the shelters."

Gene remembered Fingono's Trap and said, "I'll tell you what. You call and get all the particulars and let me know when you've got everyone on board, and then I'll get all that done." They all slapped high fives, and the issue was never discussed again. Gene had learned that talk isn't a commitment. Without action, it's just another substitute for watching TV.

Some things you can do include committing to not talking about what others could do unless you are willing to be a part of the activity and you've been asked to give your advice. When you hear others giving such thoughts or advice, ask them point blank, "Are you willing to do that / help me / be a part of it?" And "When would *you* want to begin that?" Don't let yourself or others get away with a "drive-by shoulding."

Remember—Fingono's Trap is a trap. Once you get lured into it, you find all kinds of ways to be kept in it. Stay out of it. Take control of your life and make things happen. In other words, be actively involved. Make the effort to reach out and turn on the lights. Don't just wag your tongue and wait for the sun to dawn on you.

Cogito! If you talk about problems a lot and rarely get around to fixing them, make a contract with yourself to only gripe to one person or for ten minutes and then never speak of it again. Or as my mom used to say, "Either put up or shut up. Nobody wants to hear it." Even if they do, it still doesn't fix anything to gripe.

Relationships: In the Cogito! above, I state it doesn't fix anything to gripe. Griping alone does not do anything except help someone else feel as bad about what has happened to you as you do. Part of Fingono's Trap is believing you're not in a trap. Griping is a trap that others will defend as a strategy for relieving stress and helping you refocus through a process of getting it off your chest. This is a myth. In fact, studies going back almost thirty years show that people who gripe feel worse and for a longer period of time than do those that keep quiet and learn how to flush or download the anxiety by other means. (Note I did not say shut up and keep obsessing over it in silence. There is a big difference between what I said and this last statement.)

There are two aspects of this concept that relate to relationships. The first is the more obvious—talking to others about your issues can wear a relationship very thin. People may be very well meaning and want to help, but if you talk and talk about your problems when they are around, you may well find they avoid being around! People who like or love you want to help you feel good (or better), and they want to help you be better. As noted above, talking about an issue is only the first step. If that's the only step you take, you not only don't fix the first problem; you may be creating a new one with someone else.

The second aspect of this behavior is that the original problem remains unaddressed. In any problem-solving strategy, conversation may be useful in both defining a problem (i.e., determining exactly what makes this a problem at all) and creating a plan of action to fix it. But at some point, a problem that has no fix, no end, no action for correction is a problem that will live forever. It may look like you're done with it, but the reality is that it will likely remain simply buried like it's a dead problem, but at the first press of a relationship stressor, it will once again spring to life. I call these "vampire issues."

Drive a stake in the heart of this issue by getting past this trap. Talking about something ad infinitum is not fixing it. It can feel like it is, and it can feel like you're at least getting past it by unloading it onto someone else. That is the trap. Be aware and step out of it. It's better for you, and it's better for your relationships.

> Josh rails on to his wife that the trash collectors keep making a mess—but never calls to correct it.
>
> Loretta gripes about having to stay late at work—but never talks to her boss about it.
>
> Frank goes through a litany of problems he sees every time he goes to the store—but never brings any of it to the attention of the manager.
>
> The trap is that in each case, there is a sense or feeling of accomplishment by complaining, so nothing is ever really accomplished.

Decisions: There is a relatively new cliché: analysis paralysis. This little phrase implies that a person is stymied and stopped by a fear that he will make a mistake if he doesn't have every possible outcome in mind with every imaginable alternative considered before implementing a solution. For some, this is a real fear—and, in some cases, justified.

But, analysis paralysis implies you are at least analyzing. Fingono's Trap has you potentially believing that is what you're doing when, in fact, you really aren't doing anything but retreading the same ground over and over again. You aren't moving forward, and you aren't analyzing anything new. The trap is that it can feel as though you are. This is a difficult trap to recognize because we can always justify what we did or are doing by using the circular logic going back through the thinking that got us here to begin with.

To step out of this trap requires a conscious effort and commitment to do so. Plan an execution date, and by that I mean to tell yourself that you will do something by next Tuesday or whatever makes sense. In a way, this is an oblique way of using goal setting as a motivator to get on with it. Or limit yourself to a certain number of discussions or people with whom to speak about it, or number of alternatives about what to do.

Problem solving and decision making can begin with a conversation, but even if the best solution is to just plain forget about it and let it go, there comes a time to actually do it.

MAGARI!

Donald, a client of mine, came into my office for counseling and began to complain about his sister. "This past Saturday," he said, "we held a family gathering at our home, and my sister caught up with me in the gazebo of our backyard. It's nice, you know? We have a small brook, the little flowered footbridge, and the koi pond."

The water lapped melodiously beneath their feet. All was peaceful, serene, and stunningly beautiful—and all was his, the fruits of his many years of labor. The two of them, drinks in hand, looked silently about the verdant expanse.

Then, without any warning, his sister looked at him and said, "I could have done this too, you know."

"What are you talking about?" he asked.

"I could have made the kind of money you did, and I could have had a nice place just like this," she responded.

Donald told me that the direction of the conversation was disconcerting, and he had no interest in pursuing it, but a little gremlin inside his head was more than a little peeved, and out of his mouth came this silly, stupid, and quickly regretted retort, "Oh yeah? Then why didn't you do it?" As soon as he felt those words pass over his tongue, he knew he had made a mistake. But as we all know, once the bullet leaves the muzzle, you cannot take it back. It was now time to pay the price.

"Why?" she hissed. "I'll tell you why, Mr. Everything-I-Touch-Turns-to-Gold! It's because I wasn't as lucky as you. I didn't have the luxury of …" And we all know where that went. Finally, she got down to this. "I could have gone to school if only I had blah-blah-blah … I could have gotten my broker's license if only it wasn't yaddah-yaddah-yah … I could have … (fill in missed opportunity of choice) … if only … (fill in excuse of choice)" and the litany of reasons continued, punctuated liberally with the phrase *if only*. If only, if only, if only. Or as Leonello Baldini, an old Italian man I knew, once whimsically said with a glint in his eye and a wave of his gnarled fingers, "Magari … se solo!" If only!

143

The difference between Sr. Baldini and Donald's sister is that Leonello knew that he had made certain decisions and that he was where he was and had what he had because he had been the master of his life. It was he, Baldini himself, who had brought him to where he was in his life. His "if only" (*magari* in Italian) was not a condemnation for the vagaries of life or the world about him. To Leonello, it was an acknowledgment of the fact that there could have been any number of different outcomes in his life if *he had made different choices and decisions.* There is no one to blame—not even himself. When you accept

> To live a life by design is to look ahead of tomorrow, choose where you want your life to be or what it will look like, then do the things that will likely make that happen. It is to first take responsibility and accept that you are making your own choices. Then, it's your planning and your execution that create the future that unfolds. If you've really done your best, then if it doesn't all work out as planned, you will have not only no one to blame, you will have no need to blame anyone, not even yourself.

responsibility for living your life by design, no matter how well or poorly it turns out, there is no room for blame.

But, being fair, we all do this sometimes, don't we? I mean, don't we all occasionally look back at a time when we might have taken the road less traveled and said to ourselves with a wave of our fingers, "Magari ..."? We meet someone we almost went into partnership with, almost married, almost took off for a hike across Europe with and think "Magari ..." We've all had that wonder of how things might have been, if only. But Donald's sister was not whimsically wondering. She was enviously condemning all around her for controlling her and preventing her from reaching her full potential. And therein lies the problem. She was condemning the world, and perhaps even her brother, for the successes of others, implying that they were at the cost of her own.

Many of us never get past the fact that all of us are dealt a hand at birth. Some hands are definitely better than others for certain kinds of success. But depending on what we do or how we play our hand, so to speak, we can be successful in a way that can bring us happiness. Not all of us can have the same kinds of things, but we can almost all be happy.

Before there was radio, people were happy. Before there was TV, people were happy. Before there were cars, computers, video games, smartphones, and all the trappings of modern convenience, people were happy—and, just maybe, happier because it took less to be satisfied. So the point is that the focus of what will bring us happiness is also the basis of our level of happiness. If we insist that we must have a big house, new car, all the latest gadgets and gizmos to be happy, we set ourselves up for constant want, for there will always be new things. *If on the other hand, we find a way to allow ourselves to be happy with fewer things, we set ourselves up for greater happiness.* (Review "The First Steps" chapter for a greater insight into this last statement.)

Let's be honest with ourselves for just a minute. No one's listening to your thoughts. No one is going to ask you what

Gerta was around forty when I met her as a child in grade school. She had two kids ahead of me in the same school. She was a tall, lean, and pretty woman who never stopped smiling (at least around us).

One day she shared a story about her life that a small child like I was would never have dreamed of. She was a survivor of Auschwitz, the most infamous of the German killing camps of WWII.

She told us that every day was a gift to them. She was still a teen but knew her possible fate. They found ways to play games with pebbles and roaches. When you understand that even people in Auschwitz found a way to steal a little happiness in that truly awful environment, it frees you to find it wherever you may be. Look for it. Create it out of thin air!

you say to yourself when you answer this, so be honest without mercy. Isn't it possible for you, or me or anyone else for that matter, to be able to look at your life and think that you *could* have done more and therefore have more, that you could have had as good a job as some others and could have been as good at something as some others are—if only?

"If only I had been born less poor, if only I had been able to go to a better school, if only my parents had been better at being parents, if only my teachers didn't, if only my wife would, if only, if only, if only!" They are just two little words, but when you put them together and use them as a condemnation of your own life or to blame others for where you are or what you have, they become the core snowball rolling down a ski slope, building size and wreaking havoc all along the way. They are the seeds to the destruction of your happiness because they are the root of jealousy and even revenge.

You can be happy no matter where you are or what you have. Happiness can be seen in the face of the poorest of the poor and sickest of the sick. It is all a matter of where your head is. Donald's sister's head was in a no man's land of crushed dreams that never made it past being just that—dreams. We are the masters not of our world but of our minds, and thus our happiness. But we must be willing to let go of that which we do not have and embrace that which we do—especially the affections of those we love. Then we, too, can someday sit in utter contentment and simply muse without the smallest hint of envy as did Leonello, "Magari …"

Cogito! Shakespeare's Hamlet says, "There is nothing either good or bad, but the thinking makes it so." I agree. Are you trapped in a kind of thinking with bars made of envy, jealousy, resentment, revenge, and anger? These are all examples of that wonderful part of life called emotions. As I've been saying since the title page of this book:

Think more, feel less,
And you can find happiness
That can endure regardless
Of what you or your "brother" may possess.

Relationships: The single worst word associated with a relationship is divorce. No, I'm not referring to the legal idea of its relating to a marriage. I'm talking about a more generic understanding of the word—the idea of a separation of any two things or people. In this case, we need to step a little into the realm of the metaphorical.

Relationships are built with bonds or bridges that connect two people with something they both hold onto. If I am in love with you, and you don't even know I exist, we don't really have a relationship, for example. So, in order for a relationship to remain intact or grow, those bonds must also remain intact. Here is where the story above shows us how we can really mess things up without even trying.

Let's say that you are working for a company you aren't all that happy with, but you're doing okay, you don't hate it, and it's bearable to go to work every day. Someone meets you at a coffee shop and starts telling you about a job opening at his workplace that you would be just perfect for. You go and meet with some of the most important people in the hiring for that job, and they all love you. They show you around and introduce you to the people you would work with, and they just shower you with welcoming and fraternity. The VP tells you that you are a virtual shoe-in, and he'll be getting back with you very soon.

Wow! You are on cloud nine and can't wait to get started, but until then, you still have to show up at your old place—but something just isn't the same. Now, what was once bearable is crushing you. What you didn't particularly love, now you despise. Your paycheck seems more of an insult than an equitable exchange for your work there. You can barely force yourself to keep going.

A week goes by—then two. After almost three weeks, you call the VP, and after a three-minute wait, she answers and tells you they filled the job weeks ago and they're sorry—you would have been a great addition to their work family. They'll keep your information on file for when hell freezes over. Now what? You are now essentially in a corrupted relationship.

The only reason your relationship still exists is there are still bonds and bridges like pay, benefits, and some kind of security for you, and an acceptable output of work from you for them. This bond is thin and weak and could rupture at any time. What happened? Your unconscious mind took you from your current realm into the realm of "what if." The realm of Magari!

Once you began to see yourself in that realm, your ties to your current realm began to weaken. You began a process of emotional divorce. This is not a funny thing or a small thing. It is a major shift in your psychology, and it can completely ruin whatever good there ever was in that relationship. And it could just as easily happen in a love relationship like a marriage, if the *what if* was thinking about another person and not your current spouse.

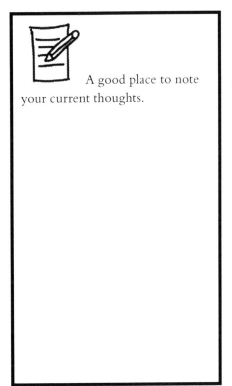

A good place to note your current thoughts.

These are dangerous waters. You can't simply float on your back and wait for things to improve. You must literally flush your mind of this whimsy and focus once again on the positives of what really is. Your emotions may have you tied in knots with resentment, anger, annoyance, and others. You may find yourself not nitpicking what was once just a minor trait or characteristic of the job, customer, or spouse. Your focus is drawn into a kind of black hole wherein there is less and less good about where you are, and the oh-so-wonderfulness of where you might have been if only!

Perhaps you've heard a few of these sayings that apply: never count your chickens before they hatch; a bird in the hand is worth two in the bush; don't spend your money until the check clears. These and many other truisms imply a long-standing comprehension of the value of not letting go of one trapeze until you have the other in your hand—so to speak. The point here is that whimsical thinking is a place where dreams are formed and ideas become plans, but it is also where alliances are formed and relationships are broken. It's about focus and balance.

But what do you do if you're already there? How do you get back to a point where the original relationship holds value for you once again? The answer, like so many in these pages, is not easily found nor known. The fact is there may be no way back to what once was. You may have burned those bridges or broken those bonds that tie. But if you are to have any hope of renewing those bonds, you must first break off all connections with the alternative draw. As a marriage counselor, I ask two questions privately of each in the couple. The first is "Do you really want to work on fixing this relationship or are you looking for a way out?" And the second is, "Are you having an affair currently?" If the answer to the second question is yes, we've got nowhere to go. Unless that is completely terminated with no chance of picking it back up, we really have no basis for moving forward together.

After you remove the temptation of an emotional affair with a person, job, customer, or object (like a flashy car or expensive guitar), you must consciously focus on what it is about that current relationship that put you there to begin with and the good things you get out of it. In other words, whether with an employer, spouse, or customer, you must go through the motion of falling in love once again. It is hard not to feel resentment and a sense of loss sometimes, but then again, that's what the rest of naked thinking is all about.

Decisions: Have you ever heard someone say, "Gee, this would be so much easier if I had an extra ten thousand to spend on this project!"? What did you say? Did you say something like, "Yeah, well we don't. So what do we do with what we *do* have?" That retort is an appeal to get back to reality and away from the whimsical. It's another way of saying get out of the realm of *if only* (or *what if*) thinking and back into the realm of the real. Psychologists might say to get out of the irrational (non-reality-based thinking) and back into the realm of the rational (or reality-based naked thinking).

Think back to when you took geometry in high school,

Today I needed things at the grocery store for making a cake. The list was long, but before I left for the store, I went through the kitchen to see what ingredients I already had so I could then buy only what I didn't have. When working any problem or issue, begin with the reality of what is and not "what if."

if you did—about what you had to do with a word problem or proof, which helped you go from the basic theorems and postulates to the logical statements you needed to solve the problem or test your hypothetical. The very first thing you were asked to do, usually anyway, was to write down all the knowns or givens. In other words, after you define what you're doing, you take stock of what you have to work with—and by "have to" I mean both "*have* to work with" and "*have to* work with."

Start there, and when an issue seems to require something more, as in any problem you might work through, consider those things that make sense and would be available if sought. Keep the three costs of time, money, and emotional currency in mind when evaluating your next step. If at any time you find yourself saying, "if only I had X" or "if only we could Y," that might be a good time to stop, distract yourself for a few minutes, and refocus on what you do have.

The 5 Percent Solution

About a mile and a half from where I live, there is a post. This post is in the middle of a path through some woods that run along the edge of our neighborhood. The post's purpose is to prevent off-road vehicles from using this paved path meant expressly for walking and running. I use it as a point around which to turn as I return to my starting point while I run (in truth, I do a lot more walking than running).

I hate running. But as I get older, it becomes increasingly important to make myself exercise, so exercise has become more important than ever—and did I mention I hate it? So, every so often, when I'm dragging my middle-aged tush through the woods to that post, the thought crosses my mind to turn around before I get that far. After all, who's going to know? I know I will, but I'm making the decision, and I don't care! So why not do it?

My answer may surprise you. It isn't, in my opinion, a big deal to cut corners with yourself if that's what you want to do. You make your rules and your own decisions, and you live with the outcome of what you do. My reason for not cutting this corner is psychological as well as physical. Let's take the second reason first.

Physically, when a person cuts corners, he or she yields to the tendencies of all living and aging things to wind down. There is a natural progression of forces constantly working to make you weaker and eventually so much so that you die. Each time you give in to them, they win a little more ground, and you'll either find it tougher to retake that ground or you never get it back at all. There is an old axiom in medicine that it's a whole lot easier to stay in shape than to get back in shape … especially once you've reached your early forties.

The psychological reasons, though, are of much greater importance. Each time I cut a corner and allow myself to less-than-finish, I become a little more used to or accepting of less-than-finished. And with each new endeavor I take on, there is a slightly lessened standard of performance to which I will hold myself. Excellence, then, becomes a point achieved only in my mind, and such a judgment of my performance will not be shared by others.

How many times have you hired a kid, a contractor, or even a purveyor of professional services, such as a lawyer or doctor, that was very excited and eager at the beginning of a project only to fizzle out at the end? A perfect example is getting a contractor to build a house for you. At the planning meeting, they're full of fire and testimonies of how they were and will be better than every other contractor that ever lived. (Rule to remember: every professional anything will always have testimonials. If you never had satisfied customers, you couldn't stay in business.)

Finally they break ground, and boy do they get that frame up in a hurry. The roof goes up, and then you notice they aren't working today—or tomorrow. You ask why, and there is a multiplicity of reasons, such as the plumbing guy is out sick, or the inspectors are on vacation. The list can be long and creative. Eventually, a closing date is agreed on, and you sell the house you're living in, and you notice your new one doesn't seem to be getting any closer to done. But the assurances keep coming. The day before closing, everyone is scurrying around to satisfy the bank and get your certificate of occupancy. "Don't worry," they say, "just make out a punch list, and we'll get it all done once you're in." When you do get in, they take care of the big stuff, but there are about a dozen smaller things that will never, ever get done.

A close look at the process will show that this is a pattern that is repeated in almost any walk of life or endeavor involving human beings. People tend to be interested in doing a good job at the beginning and lose interest toward the finish. (Have you ever noticed how much more toothpaste you need to brush your teeth at the beginning of a tube than the very end of a tube, especially when you keep forgetting to buy another?) But you judge the excellence of any project by the final 5 percent, not the first 95. Why? Because that last five is what you (or your customers) live with.

Anyone can start a project. Many of us are really, really good at it. In fact, we start new ones all the time. What makes someone exceptional isn't that he can start a project, it's how he finishes the ones he starts. To finish as well as you start takes what I call character. I define character like this:

Character: The ability to keep your commitments long after the emotion of the moment in which you made the commitment has passed. That is, while it's easy to make a commitment when you are caught up in an emotion such as love or enthusiasm, it takes character to keep those commitments when the first blush is over.

Do a personal analysis. Are you a person who starts with great enthusiasm and then, before you're done, find yourself starting another project, leaving the first unfinished? If you, like I and almost everyone else in the universe, fall into this category, the answer isn't in making smaller promises or taking on smaller projects. No matter how large or small the commitment, the result will always be the same. The last little bit will lose your interest as you move on to the next thing.

The better thing to do is find a built-in incentive to keep your interest in finishing. For example, don't cash the final check until you've finished the final task. Whatever it takes, it starts with knowing this important characteristic about yourself and doing something about it. It is that last 5 percent that makes the difference between very good and excellent.

It seemed as though it was only a post along a lonely path through the woods at the edge of a neighborhood. But as you can see, it's really a marker along a path to excellence. If you want to be good, or even really good, cut some corners. If you want to be truly great and create excellence in the minds of others as well as your own, then round every post along your path and focus on that last 5 percent—even when no one else is looking.

Cogito! Anyone can say anything. To borrow from Bacall, just put your lips together and blow. But you are eventually judged by what you do—not only by others but also by yourself. Following your emotions means to say yes if you're excited. Following your head is to say no, even if it's difficult, if it's the best decision to make. So use your naked thinking and always be considerate before making a commitment.

Then keep that commitment as though your very life depends on it. In a metaphorical sense, it does.

Relationships: Every relationship requires the ability to count on the other party in some way or another. When you continue to not do what you promise, it's a little like trying to stand still while on the beach with the waves constantly moving the sand under your feet. Over time, people begin to see you as unreliable and automatically begin to dismiss you or work around you. Making promises to others is seen as hollow or, worse, dishonest.

As stated in the chapter "Trust Is Never Earned," you will recall that to trust someone requires motivation to do so. If you make promises or commitments and then only start and often don't finish, their motivation isn't to trust you; it's to manage you—handle you. This begins to erode the relationship and change its nature. What may have at one time been a relationship of sharing secrets and dreams is now one of perfunctory civility and the minimum to get along. In the workplace, resentments and a sense of being dismissed or taken advantage of may develop. Along with that, a taste for revenge by sabotaging your other efforts may begin to grow.

If you are prone to make commitments or promises when in the throes of an emotion, such as remorse, shame, guilt, enthusiasm, joy, and so on, you will want to put some kind of governing mechanism in place. Learn how to say something that buys you enough time to allow the emotions of the moment to pass. For example, learn how to automatically say something like, "Wow! That sounds great! Let me think about it, and I'll get back to you tomorrow." When asked why you can't go ahead and say yes, have another ready response in your repertoire like, "I'm inclined to want to do this, but I don't want to say yes now and discover that I can't follow through." If, like many salespeople do, they then say, "Well let's go ahead and put you down as a yes, and you can cancel if you need to," you would likely now be feeling something.

This emotion will have a power of pressure that might make you capitulate. Now is the time to become a little more assertive and just say, "No. That's not how I like to do things. If I have to give you an answer now, it's no. If you can give me the time I need to carefully consider it, then it's maybe."

Some consider that being a smart aleck. That in itself is a pressure to not do this. Naked thinking is expressly for times like these. That is, it's at times like this in a relationship we will say yes or no to things when an hour from now in the quiet of our own thoughts, we will come to think better of it. Rather than yield or succumb to the pressure of the emotions of the moment, have a repertoire of ready responses that fit your personality and practice saying them! I know that sounds weird, but it's going to sound weird whenever you do it the first few times. If you practice out loud to yourself several times first, it will at least feel more comfortable and not add to the pressure to commit when you shouldn't.

Decisions: In decision making, a great problem arises from the pressure of what is motivating you to make the decision. It is common for a problem state or a desire for something to initiate the need to make such a decision. As time goes by, it is also common for that pressure to take a backseat to other things, so that what at one time seemed so important to decide is now not really that important.

Step one of any problem-solving process, as stated already, is to evaluate whether the decision is really something you need to do. If the answer was yes, then no matter what your current emotional state, finish it out to the bitter end. If you're working with others, it will instill in them that reason to trust you in the future and take you seriously. If you're on your own, then your own sense of efficacy and honor will be underpinned. Both are crucial and pave the road for future success even if this issue has lost its importance.

Just over the Next Horizon

From deep in the Rocky Mountains, there is a story of a man that spent years with his pick, scrounging in the dirt, looking for a gold vein that he believed to be where he was looking. Day after day, year after year, he plunged his pick into the earth only to come up with nothing to show for it but a sore back. Finally, one day in a fit of disgust, he thrust his pick into the ground so hard the handle broke. With that, the man left, never to return, leaving the pick where it lay. Years later, just six feet from where the pick head was still buried in the dirt, one of the richest gold veins ever found was uncovered.

The moral of the story, it would seem of course, is to never give up—never, ever give up. To many motivators, the message is simple: "Don't ever give up on your dreams, no matter how impossible they may seem!" But as you may have guessed, my message isn't like most other motivators'. My message is *sometimes it makes better sense to give up on a lost cause and move on to things that you can conquer.* Emotions will stop you. Naked thinking moves you.

Recently, I went to a movie wherein someone made the statement that a person's greatness isn't shown by the talents he possesses but by the choices he (or she) makes. And that's what this prospector story is really all about. Truly successful people aren't those that just keep on battling against the odds. Truly successful people weigh the odds, make a choice, and pursue their goals with a dogged determination to succeed. All the while, though, they are educating themselves about what they're doing, and every day they are making a decision to continue their efforts, or stop and move on to other things.

Think of how much misery is gained by not letting go of an idea or ideal that gets caught in your head. As a therapist, I had a client that sat on my couch and told me that she was attending a nursing school class that she had herself taught years before. After four classes, she realized that she knew the material inside out. She hated the teacher, and it was from seven to ten o'clock at night during the winter and therefore was depressing to attend as well. And further, there were no continuing education credits to be gained, and her employer didn't even know she was going.

I asked her if this meant she was going to stop going. Emphatically, she said no. Puzzled, I asked why not. Her response was that she had signed up, told herself she was going to attend, had started going, and by golly she was going to finish anything she started no matter how worthless it was to her. In other words, once you begin, never give up—never, ever give up! And she went on to be miserable three times a week for the next three months. (When it was over, she had a book-burning ceremony with a friend because she hated the course so much.)

We only get a certain amount of time and energy to spend before we must shuffle off this mortal coil. Taking on what seems to be impossible challenges is exciting and gives us a real sense of purpose. And when we beat the odds and make what seems to be impossible happen, it gives most of us a thrill of accomplishment that cannot be matched. But the world is full of difficult challenges. There is a never-ending supply of things we can do and accomplish if we put our minds and hearts into it. What that means is that there is no reason to spend ourselves empty with something that will (or likely will) never happen.

You've heard it, that way some people (including yourself) keep you on the hook. It sounds like this: "Don't give up now! It'll be just a little longer. Trust me. Success is just around the next corner, just behind the next rock, just over the next horizon." Gamblers (and owners of stocks) use this thinking when they're losing. They keep on playing, continuing to lose, expecting their luck to turn and win back what they lost. This is called chasing your losses and is by all standards a fool's bet. The psychological snare is that sometimes continuous, persistent pursuit does occasionally yield results that can be quite rewarding. This variable reinforcement is the same thing that keeps someone in a devastating relationship with a drunk or physically abusive person. Every so many weekends, and unpredictably so, this person is the person you fell in love with, so you constantly think, *If I just hang in there a little longer, I'm sure his changing back into his wonderful true self is just over the next horizon.* Your own experience tells you it rarely really happens like that.

The bottom line is easy to discern:

1. Choose your challenges when you can.
2. Evaluate what you're doing to overcome the obstacles.

3. Be willing to change your method of operation when evidence shows that there may be a better way.

> Dave wanted to quit his job and become a professional street performer and then move up to working clubs. He played guitar a little, and his singing was unique.
>
> After four months and eight chances to get feedback for his work, the public seemed completely indifferent to him, and he never made more than three dollars a day. His dilemma was: should he quit his day job and move to NYC so more people could see him, or would it be better to work on his skills, keep his current employment, and leave his hobby a hobby.
>
> Only he could decide, but this is a prime example of when it might be a good time to change your dream to something more achievable.

And, perhaps maybe above all else, be willing to let go of a great idea when it shows itself to be a bad goal.

There will always be things you can do and accomplish—difficult, worthwhile things. So nothing you take on is the be-all and end-all of who or what you are. There will always be, just over the next horizon, another challenge ready for you to meet, so spend your talents and energies wisely. And remember the earth is round; there will always be a next horizon.

Cogito! If you use naked thinking and not feeling as your guide to success, then your plans will include a limited amount of time, money, and emotional currency you will put into it. When you've expended your limit, don't feel—think. Just plain old follow through with your plan and don't look back except to learn from it. If you do this, there will be no regrets, just occasional disappointments.

Relationships: In relationships that we deem to be particularly important (such as a marriage, family tie, business partner, or valued customer), we often use wishful thinking as a basis for judging how things are going. We want things to work out so badly we make excuses for what doesn't work or dismiss any evidence that the relationship is no longer yielding its intended goodness. This is a terrible place to be, yet it is a common place to be as well.

Like in the gold vein story, we have the problem that, every so often, we get a small nugget of what we want, and so we keep mining. But some mines (relationships) are really spent, and no amount of digging is going to reawaken it. That's when it makes sense to accept the way things are and move on.

This is hard, of course. The biggest reason is that it feels bad to do it! You may love that person oh, so much! You may believe you will never find another customer as good as this one was. Or the dissolution of the relationship will require a lot of doing with paperwork, legal issues, and financial costs, and so you dread the process less than the outcome. All of these emotional reactions to the loss of a dead relationship are reasonable and normal. That doesn't make them any less of a stumbling block to a better decision and a better future.

Naked thinking is required most when your emotions are at their greatest! Remember—emotions are a part of everyday living. We aren't trying to find a way to eliminate them. What we're after is finding a way to tame them so we can more clearly think through the evaluation process and then make a decision that will stand the test of time—that is, the time of the passing of the current state of emotions.

Consider how many times you've said or done something that as little as a few minutes later you've thought to yourself, *Oh man! I coulda said—I shoulda done—if I had thought of it, I woulda.* The test of time is based on whether or not, after the emotions of the moment have passed, will you be in a position to woulda, coulda, shoulda on yourself.

If every time you think about the value of terminating a relationship, you find yourself feeling depressed, anxious, guilty, ashamed, or any other strong emotion, seek the help of a friend or a professional, such as a counselor or consultant. It's hard for everyone to do this. Give yourself the best shot at cutting your losses and moving forward and don't give in to the allure of thinking that things will get better on their own or that a change for the better is just over the next horizon.

Decisions: In decision making, we are faced with what psychologists might refer to as a double bind—that is, a situation in which a person is confronted with two irreconcilable demands or a choice between two undesirable courses of action. If we are confronted with having to make a decision that affects others, as in a professional capacity for example, we are expected to do our due diligence in the process of making it. Therein is the bind or confrontation between two seemingly irreconcilable demands and maybe even two undesirable courses of action.

On the one hand, you are expected to seek all the information possible to make a valid and useful decision but not take so long as to be rendered impotent and indecisive altogether. Often, the decision may be to completely undo all that's been done on a particular project already, making it seem as though you've wasted a huge amount of time and resources up till now. Oh, brother! What a mess! To stop is to admit fault; to continue is to go even farther in a hole. There's no wonder your mind looks for reasons to assuage and comfort you with the idea that if you just close your eyes, click your heels three times, and pretend it isn't happening, things will take care of themselves. And, of course, sometimes they do!

This is where the rubber meets the road in naked thinking. This is a tough one. It requires a great deal of personal integrity and character to suck it up and do what is right regardless of how it looks. Remember my definition of courage: the ability to stand up to any strong emotion and still do what you know is right anyway. But how? How do you find that courage and distinguish it from another underlying emotional trap of just wanting to get out from under a mess and be done with it, and this is a way to do it? (And people think managers make a lot of money doing nothing but walking around with their hands in their pockets while making everyone else really work.)

Use the following as a sticking post and screw your courage to that sticking post, and you will not fail. Begin with what outcome you want. Look then at the criteria you'll use to know you've arrived and have created that outcome successfully. Next, compare where your current course of action is taking you to where you want it to. Finally, use the cost-benefit analysis with time, money, and emotional currency (and in some cases, opportunity cost of not doing something else). Whatever your analysis tells you is what is and not necessarily what you'd like it to be. If it's not taking you where you need to go, then, well, that's where it's up to you to decide. Just don't get caught up with the avoidance strategy of telling yourself your analysis is wrong and that success is just around the corner or just over the next horizon.

GET OVER IT

Recently, I had the occasion to be reintroduced to the concept of something referred to by some as "emotional intelligence" and EQ (emotional quotient). To me, emotional intelligence means to be intelligent enough to understand the true nature of emotions and how they relate to the world of reality and reason, and to be intelligent enough about your emotions to not be run by them. They tell you nothing about the real world or what is true and correct in your universe.

Is it all right to feel emotions when things happen? Am I saying that you shouldn't feel at all when important things occur? Are you supposed to be like a robot when you face difficulties? Of course the answers are self-evident and discussed at length in section 1 of this book. If you don't remember and they are not so self-evident, go back and review the myths outlined.

You have a right to feel any way you want at any time about anything. But if you want to make good decisions that you can live with when the emotion passes, then you will want to give yourself enough time and distance from the event as possible and feel as little and think as much as you can—that is, tame your emotions and focus your thinking. Whether that's culturally out of step today or not, it's still the best way to make decisions.

Keep a few axioms and witticisms of the past in mind.

- Let cooler heads prevail.
- Time heals all wounds.
- A word spoken in anger will be the worst speech you ever regret.
- Look before you leap.
- Haste makes waste.
- Don't just do something; stand there!

All of these refer to one simple truth: it makes greater sense to allow your feelings to abate and give yourself time to think before doing anything of consequence. Knowing that your feelings can drag you off in any direction and refusing to be is the very essence of naked thinking and a key ingredient to making a good decision you will never regret.

As you gain greater control of your emotions, you will find you can more effectively use your best talents of thinking and decision making. And you can appraise how well you're doing by using what I call your Get-over-it Quotient (GOI-Q) as a measuring guide. Of course, there is no such thing precisely, but you can think of it as a type of scale for comparison and how far along on that scale you are today versus yesterday. For example, you could say that you're being like a Mr. Spock from *Star Trek* is a ten on your scale. Your being totally stopped by your emotions is a one (as in being enraged, phobic, or profoundly depressed). In a clinical setting with a psychologist, it is akin to what is called a SUDS or a "subjective unit of distress scale" where a ten might be very happy and calm, and a one is completely upset or depressed.

As you begin, you might think you're at a three and would like to be more of an eight. As you read on and practice letting things go, you can then stop occasionally and reevaluate to see your progress. If you believe you're not making much, it might be a good time to talk to a counselor, someone you've confided in, or a coach. If you believe you've made some progress, you can then redouble your efforts and use that progress as a basis for greater motivation. Remember that this isn't robot or doormat training. It is simply one of the best ways there is to tame your emotions and engage the power of your intellect when it is important to do so.

Remember you are in control of your life. Be in better control of your emotions and you'll make better decisions and feel even better as a result. Or as I like to put it, GOI-GOWI (get over it-get on with it)!

Cogito! Remember almost all animals can feel something, even if it's just fear or anger. Emotions aren't what make us human. It is our thoughts that distinguish us from the rest of the animal kingdom. And it's thinking—not feeling an emotion—that built the pyramids and sent men to the moon. Emotions are like gasoline in that in the rawest of forms it'll burn weak and warm. When contained in an engine, it will be the power to move freight trains. Thinking is that engine.

Relationships: Every relationship costs us something in time, money, or emotional currency. If we get enough back, we stay in that relationship. If we only give and give and get little in return, and the costs become too great, it is self-defeating to keep going on with it.

This is not to say that you are consciously and deliberately setting out to punish someone for what they've already done and will likely never do again. What it is, though, is a way of making the other party aware that they, too, are paying a price for what they've done. That is, they are working toward diminishing the value of the relationship and may well kill it.

If you're married, you have a responsibility to keep the other party aware of this erosion of value for the relationship as you go. What happens all too often is that one of the two continues to be aggrieved and never says much, but inside, they are harboring bad feelings or they're feeling less and less love for the other. They ruminate over their treatment and begin to feed an emotional stew pot that is filling to the boil-over point and never say a word. Then, one day, they realize there is so little value left, that the relationship is no longer worth the effort, and the break completely kills the relationship and any basis or hope for fixing or even saving it.

This is just as true for relationships with your children and coworkers. There are cost limits in every relationship. Contrary to the feel-good mythology of recent history, there is no such thing as unconditional love. To love unconditionally is a sign of a shattered ego and a self-defeating personality. Naked thinking and raising your GOI-Q is about having a response that is reasonable and taking the steps needed to keep your relationships on a successful track.

Decisions: There is nothing quite like having to work cooperatively with someone you detest! But in the real world of work and family, we may have to do just that. Raising your GOI-Q doesn't take all the acid reflux out of it, but it allows you to find a way to swallow hard, take a deep breath, and get on with what must be accomplished.

In decision making, we often find we have to not only work with others that trip our triggers; we have to count on them for a successful outcome. Selling your ideas to such a person requires that you find a way of putting yesterday away and moving on to tomorrow. As a way of doing that, it makes sense to focus more on the issues and not on the person. Don't dismiss what you know about that person, but don't allow yourself to be a slave to your preconceived notions or expectations.

Perchance To Dream

The old man held the boy in his arms as the youth spoke through his gasps for air. "Someday, Grandpa, when all this is over, I'm going to go back to school and become a doctor. I want to help others with leukemia so they won't have to go through what I am."

The man looked down and wiped his tears off the boy's face and said, "Someday you will. There are no expiration dates on dreams." And it was then he noticed the boy had breathed his last.

I told this story to an audience in Dallas. Just in front of me in the second row, a lady had her hands over her face, showing only her reddened eyes. I asked her what she thought the moral of the story is. With a strained and carefully controlled voice, she told me that it was obvious, that no matter what, your dreams can always be achieved, if you just never give up on them. I gave a three-second pause and quietly asked the audience for a show of hands for those that agreed. It was nearly unanimous. And everyone was wrong!

The moral of the story is not that every dream does not have an expiration date. The moral is that every wish and want, every hope and plan, will someday, by virtue of the passage of time and its attendant changes, become unachievable, and so everything does have an expiration date. To this, some flinch and say, "What an awful, un-motivational thing for a motivational speaker to say!" To which I respond, "Au contraire!"

One of the problems with humans is that we are pulled in many directions by the comings and goings of our emotions. During the course of a day or week, we come to feel as though we need or want to do something. The catch is our feelings will always change, and we are left with what we've said or done when we had those emotions.

What were you just thinking? Make a note.

Perhaps during one of those moments, we decided we wanted to achieve something specific, like becoming a doctor. After careful thought, we elevate that thought to more than a passing fancy, and it becomes a dream or wish. We may then even tell others of our desire. For many, our telling others creates for us a self-image of a thing in progress. In the example, that would be a "doctor in the making."

The more we talk about it, the more it becomes us. We begin to think of ourselves as what some day we want to be or do. Others begin to incorporate our wish into their image of us. And all the while, time keeps going.

We become older. Opportunities come and go. Our responsibilities increase or lessen. Our financial status fluctuates up or down or goes nowhere—and time keeps ticking away.

Then one day, we decide to plunk down our money and sign up for med school. And they tell us that they don't take forty-seven-year-old students that graduated from college twenty-five years before. And we realize it's too late. Indeed, our dream has expired.

It's been said that death is our destruction and death is our salvation (I know because I said it). It is our destruction because our corporal existence does really end and we then become no more. But the knowledge that we only have a certain amount of time gives us a reason, a motivation, to act now, for no one knows how many grains of sand yet remain in our hourglass of life.

Hope is a great salve. It helps to get us through tough times and gives us something to focus on when the present is frightening. But as my mom used to say, hope doesn't feed the house cat—getting off the dime, going to the pantry, taking out the bag, and pouring food into the bowl does. In other words, dreams without action are no more than the visions we see in the clouds as they pass overhead. Sure, they're nice to look at and talk about at parties, but they have little to do with reality.

So what is the moral of the story? If you have someone special in your life and haven't told them that they are, if you have something that you want to do or accomplish, if there is something that is important to you that requires action to make it happen, do it now. And don't ever believe the sweet sentiment of the old man, no matter how comforting it is to hear it. Dreams do have expiration dates. Use yours before it's too late.

Cogito! A goal without a time limitation is not a goal. It's a wish or a whim—maybe even a fancy. If there is something you wish to do, and I mean really do, attach a time to it and make it happen. Anyone can dream and move their lips. Things get done only when you do them.

Relationships: First, if you love someone, put this down and tell them right now, even if it's just an e-mail. Can you tell someone you love too often? Well, maybe. That will depend on the people involved. But as a person and a marriage counselor, I can tell you that being told you are loved has never been a reason to go to seek help.

But there is more to this than simply telling someone you love them, especially if that relationship is with your boss, coworker, or customer. This story and the point contained within it isn't about making sure others know you care about them. It's about getting on with whatever your mind has told you is important to do or accomplish.

Dreams are usually associated with a window of time wherein one might reasonably expect to make them become a reality. As we all know, time slips by so fast, we sometimes wonder if we've been like Rip Van Winkle and fell asleep while the years kept going. You will recall the old Latin adage, tempus fugit, which is often translated as "time flies." But this is incorrect. It really means "time flees or escapes." And if your relationship requires your doing something or changing something, you may very well find that your window of opportunity to fix or enhance that relationship has closed.

Review the top four relationships in your life. Think in terms of what you might or must do in order to make that relationship what you want it to look like in one month. Formulate what you must do in order for that to happen and then do it. Do it today.

Decisions: Have you ever received a contract from a vendor that would lock you in with a certain price or policy, but you must respond within ten days (or some other short time frame)? Did you place that off to the side and figure it was a good deal but maybe you could find a better one? Then, three weeks later you rediscover the paperwork on the corner of your desk, call the vendor, and try to get the original deal, only to be told, "Sorry. That deal's expired."?

Some deals come with an expiration date in order to encourage a sense of urgency so you will be motivated to go ahead and act. But many things we think to do don't have given expiration dates, so we keep pushing them off to the corner of our desk and one day discover it's too late to do anything with it.

Decisions that are important are important because they carry with them some outcome that matters. It might matter to your spouse or a boss, or just to you. But if it doesn't really matter to anyone, it isn't really an important decision and so isn't what we're talking about here. Given that you've already qualified your issue as important, it is also important to be keenly aware of what the passage of time will do to your issue and the universe of possible alternatives. Sometimes time itself eliminates some of the best choices for resolving a problem or effecting a positive result through your decision.

A hidden drag on some people is complacency. Most wouldn't think of complacency as such, but it can be an emotional response to an issue. It's not an intense emotion, so it's hard to realize it's even at play. That sense of urgency just isn't there, and so you feel comfortable with pushing it off to another day. But sometimes, pushing off a decision allows the issue to resolve itself in a manner you might not like. Or it might force others to act around you, and that can be the worst outcome you could have.

People won't wait forever for you to fish or cut bait. They rely on you for a reason. It might be because your position requires it of you. It might be because you have promised you would take on something voluntarily. It might be something that only you can do and they have no choice but to wait on you to decide. In any event, eventually others' patience can run out and leave you with an entirely new set of problems to deal with.

Naked thinking allows you to go through the options and evaluate what needs to be done now and what can wait. It also allows you to go ahead and schedule a time on your calendar to address the problem at a specific time, rather than just go with the flow until the pressure of others is so intense you must act. Change your need to act into a goal by attaching urgency and a time frame to it. Making such a decision under pressure can very often limit your choices or your ability to think it through properly. Time takes its toll.

OF ALBATROSSES AND TREE STUMPS—A FABLE

There was a certain man sitting on a tree stump in a lonely neck of woods at the edge of a park near a downtown section of a city. His clothing was of reasonable quality but dirty and beginning to wear. His hair was greasy and uncombed. His beard looked to be several days old and unkempt. His eyes appeared almost dead, and the look on his face was one of despair.

A man who works in an office in that city took a walk through those woods during lunchtime and found the man sitting on the tree stump just staring off into space. The lunch walker went up to the stump sitter and began a conversation.

"Are you all right? You look lost or ill."

The stump sitter replied, "I'm not ill, but I am not all right."

Taking the answer as too enigmatic to ignore, the walker continued. "If you are not ill, what is it that's bothering you? Can I be of help?"

"You had better stay away from me. I'm bad luck. Very bad luck, indeed. If you don't want your life to become a real mess, you had better keep on moving and forget you've ever even seen me."

Finding the enigma wrapped in a confusion, the walker pressed on. "How can someone be bad luck? Are you saying that simply having spoken to you or knowing you is a cause for the fates to exact some kind of mischief on me?"

"I can't say I know what fate will do. In fact, I am completely without a clue as to what fate even might do. It would seem that each time I thought I did know, it proved that I was living in a fool's paradise and really knew nothing at all about fate, the future, or what it takes to create success. Evidently, I am like that ancient traveler cursed by a god and forever followed by failure and tragedy. So if you want to escape my fate, you'd better keep on walking and forget you ever met me."

"I don't mean to pry into your business—after all, you seem to be perturbed enough without a stranger meddling in your life—but you seem so morose, yet there is a spark in your speech that tells me that you are no failure at all. And yet still, here you sit with what seems to be the weight of the universe pressing down on your mind. Please indulge my curiosity and desire to help by telling me what it is that's happened to you and places you here on this stump."

And like an ancient mariner, the stump sitter began his tale. "I was just like you not more than a few months ago. I had a job, benefits, a wife, kids, and a house with the usual trappings of mediocrity. My job was mediocre, my marriage was mediocre, my life was just like everyone else's … very, very average—that is, mediocre.

"I found myself wanting more out of life. I began to focus on what I did not have and what I had not accomplished and began to disdain my life so much that I became miserable with my miserable, average life. I became disdainful in my speech to my wife and children. I spoke disdainfully to my dog and to my colleagues of mediocrity at work. And I spoke disdainfully to myself within the mediocre mind that is behind my own eyes. In other words, even though I was living what most would see as a successful life and nothing in it had changed from what it was a few months or years before, I found myself more and more miserable with it."

"If I might interrupt you for just a moment," the walker interjected, "what you just said is that your life really didn't change at all, but you found the way you were living becoming more and more intolerable. Is that what you said?"

"Oh, that seems so clear now as you say it, but at the time of this evolution, it seemed clear to me that my life was sliding into a black hole and that I was being inexorably drawn into the abyss by an outside force. To me then, it seemed that my life was changing all the time, and always to the worse. It seemed no matter how much I railed against it and complained, there was nothing retrievably good in it.

"Then, one day, I found myself standing over my bathroom sink, staring down the drain. I lifted my head and saw this pair of black eyes glaring back at me with just the slightest smirk across them. There seemed to be a different man behind those eyes than what was behind mine. And in an instant, that man was within me.

"He took me over. He began to scheme and plan and create all kinds of ways of breaking out of the mediocre and leaping into the exceptional.

He became me, and I became him. And together, we—that is, I—began to see everything and everyone as an opportunity. Each person and event was another thing I could use to climb out of this deep ravine and climb to the highest peak. Each scheme, each idea claimed its own path, leaving all else behind, as I was to find a new and better self-creation.

"But with each new path, there was also a cost. In each case, there was the loss of what I already had. There was the potential for falling so much deeper than I already had. What point would there be in blundering forward only to find the ground under my feet not there and falling into a bottomless pit? With each new thought of success, there was a new thought of even greater failure.

"Ideas, ideas everywhere,
And how they made me fear.

"Ideas, ideas everywhere,
Their failure had no peer!

"It seemed that each time I created a way to succeed, it really created a new way for me to measure my own failure! If I did *this*, I told myself, I would surely lose *that*. If I did *that*, I argued with myself, I would certainly foul up *this*. And on and on and on. It seemed that there was no good way to go, and I certainly couldn't keep going where I was going already. My only logical choice was to stop altogether and do nothing. And nothing is what I did.

"For weeks I did nothing. I got up and sat. I ate little and went to sleep often. My wife began to berate my queer method of achieving success. But for once, I thought, I was the ultimate success. I had designed a life of doing nothing, and I was very successful at doing nothing.

"Ideas, ideas everywhere,
And how they made me fear.

"Ideas, ideas everywhere,
Their failure had no peer!

"Before long, my mortgage defaulted, and we were evicted. My wife moved in with her sister, and my kids won't even speak to me. My employer sent me a brochure for the company psychiatrist along with my termination notice. My car sits on a repo lot, and my parents have asked me to start using a new last name.

"So as you can see, some god has it in for me. Too bad it wasn't Poseidon; at least I could have avoided water. Whoever it is, whether it is a god or luck or fate or whatever, even doing nothing doesn't seem to help. In other words, I must be damned, jinxed, or otherwise at odds with nature. So, as I said before, you'd better just keep on walking and forget you ever saw me."

The lunch walker shook his head in pity. "You certainly seem to be a man in a desperate state. But I don't think there is any force out there trying to get you." As he finished this statement, he reached for his wallet and opened it in front of the stump sitter. He pulled out a stack of bills, all at least denominations of twenty or more.

The stump sitter said, "Oh, no. I will not take your money. My story was told only because you insisted on it being told to satisfy your curiosity. It was for you, not for me that I've told you what happened."

The lunch walker continued to rifle through his cash. "I have no intention of giving you money. In your present state, you'd only spend it on food or something. What good is that? You'd only just get hungry again in a few hours. I have something of much greater value than cash to offer."

And as he spoke, he pulled from his bills a business card and put his wallet away. With this, he proceeded to say, "Some time ago, I too found another voice speaking to me from behind my eyes. It told me of my own inadequacies and my failures, even when I looked about and saw a wife that loved me and children that couldn't wait for me to come home. And I, too, one day found myself sitting on a sort of stump, speaking to another of such things as you did to me today. And he said not a word at all to me but rather gave me this card and left me to ponder its meaning. And I give it to you today."

The walker handed the card to the sitter, and on the card was nothing but this:

Nine words to live by: *you always get a result from whatever you do.*

Life has a beginning and an end. Everything in between is a result of everything we do beforehand. What will happen to me tomorrow is a result of what I do today. I cannot be run over by a bus in Albuquerque tomorrow if I fly to Paris today. Whatever we experience, it is a result of what we've done every yesterday we've ever lived.

Ah, the catch though is that we do not live alone or in a vacuum. We are a part of an entire world full of disease, sunshine, bugs, beauty, weather, people, and an infinite host of other things. Each and every thing has its own effect on our present moment along with the impact we have on ourselves. But the saving grace of it all is that we are not inanimate objects like rocks that are simply worn down by the passage of time. We have our thoughts, our passions, our choice and free will to act. In other words, we have a greater chance to influence our world, most of the time, than it has on us.

As a result, this gives us two wonderful things. One is the chance to make of our lives what we want; the second is the responsibility to make of our lives what we want. And you cannot abdicate your responsibilities. As the stump sitter in the story found out, you always get a result from whatever you do, and you never do nothing. There is no such thing as doing nothing. If you take a step, you're doing something. If you don't take a step, you are still doing something—that is, *not* taking a step.

There is never a time in your life when you can just sit out a few innings. You are always in the game. There are no time-outs. There are no do-overs. You always get a result from whatever you do, so always do what will give you the result you want. Never expect fate or the good graces of Apollo, Poseidon, or Wyrd to drop success in your lap. It's already there.

What does that mean? *There is no such thing as failure or success except in the mind of the person who defines it.* Each and every day, you are a success or failure depending on what you use as a measuring stick. In other words, *if you want to be a success, redefine failure.*

There will always be others out there who do not agree with what you call success. For that reason, your definition must be your own and based on your own reasons, so when others support them, it is nice, and when others denigrate them, it is annoying. But in neither case does it change your path to success.

We only get this one life on earth to get out of it what we want. If we are grounded in our morality, ethic, or dream, everything we do should be consistent with it. And if others don't agree, then we face that consequence as well. Whatever we do or however we decide to live our lives, it is our choice. It is our path. But every step or non-step is our responsibility.

And never forget that everything you do will get you some kind of result, and there is no such thing as doing nothing.

Cogito! Never believe you're taking a breather from you goals. Every day of playing on vacation is a day of delay and perhaps a first step on a new path. There is nothing wrong with that, in my opinion. The problem is when we think standing still is an alternative to moving forward or back. It is just another spot along the path. Naked thinking allows us the freedom to understand that and to not be afraid of it or to admit it. Take it for what it is and use it as the magic wand it becomes.

Relationships: You always get a result from whatever you do. That means it is a good idea to know exactly what result you want in a relationship before doing anything. Keep in mind that *not* seeing or talking to someone is *not seeing* or *not talking* to someone. As you already know very well, not talking to someone when they want or need you to can have some dramatic consequences.

If your spouse passes near you, do you touch her? When your kids are watching TV as you walk through, do you talk to them, ask them how their day is going? Do you speak to your customers or coworkers with the least speech needed to get the job done, or tell them your most intimate details whether they want to know or not? You always get a result from whatever you do, so knowing what result you want should direct what you do.

Final thing to keep in mind. Nice people *do nice things.*

Decisions: One of the least useful things added to the mix of decision making over the last few years is the concept of using "doing nothing" as an alternative in problem-solving. You never do nothing. In this case, doing nothing means to continue doing what you currently are. But you really no longer continue to do what you already are because now you also know you are! The very conversation that yielded the *do nothing* alternative course of action means you have already changed the system from what was to something else. To do nothing now that you and everyone else knows you're doing nothing is no longer doing nothing.

This is one of those "Oh, crud!" moments like when you've been discovered in some kind of situation. It isn't that you've done something wrong or bad, but now they know you did or will be doing what they discovered you doing. At this point, you face a decision to continue or to stop. Either is doing something, and neither is doing nothing. With that in mind, every action in decision making needs to be deliberate and directed to a desired outcome. If continuing to do what has been done is your chosen course, since it is now after this process has begun, it makes sense that continuing doing this nothing would include ongoing monitoring (which is doing something) to be sure your present course remains the best course.

YOU ARE THE MANAGER
OF AT LEAST ONE

If you are a manager, raise your hand. If your hand isn't up, you're wrong. Each and every one of us is the manager of at least one. You may think, *Ooooh, I am the manager of me! What a clever thing to say.* I agree … that would be the kind of lame corporate trainer thing to say that would be worthy of a skewering by Dilbert.

What I mean when I say that you are the manager of at least one is that you manage your manager, your kid, your spouse, girlfriend or boyfriend, your coworker, and yes, you do manage yourself in some ways. Many would contest the previous statement because they don't think they manage others. I'll stand by my statement and challenge you to consider just the idea that you manage at least your manager (if you work at home, pick a family member and apply the following example).

If you don't think you manage what your boss does or how he or she acts, try this someday (but not in real life). One day, when things are really busy (don't really try this), get a magazine out. When I say a magazine, I mean one of those trashy good-for-nothing magazines that can't possibly be seen as beneficial to the job. Take out this magazine (don't really try this), catch your boss's eye (don't

Nancy was a manager at a veterinary clinic. Sabrina was an assistant. Part of Sabrina's job description was to set up coffee in the waiting area every morning before they opened and keep the coffeepot clean and full until 11:00. She just didn't do it. Nancy would speak to her every few days but inevitably would wind up doing it herself or it wouldn't get done. The vet herself wanted to fire Sabrina, but Nancy made a bargain between Sabrina and Charles to swap a different duty for the coffee. After a week, Sabrina was doing neither the coffee duty nor the other. This is a simple matter that Sabrina was not going to do what she didn't want to do. The only explanation is she didn't do what she agreed to or it can be simply called a performance problem—she didn't perform as agreed. She was terminated, and someone who did all the job requirements was hired.

really do this), and sit back and begin thumbing through it (don't really try this).

When the boss comes over to you and asks what you're doing (don't really say this), look that boss square in the eye, flip a page loudly, and say (not really), "I'm reading. What'zit look like I'm doing?" (Don't really do this.) If you were to really do this (don't!), don't you think you would get a very predictable response from that boss? I think so.

So knowing that, you don't do that. You do other things because you don't want that response. That means that every day you are managing how your boss treats you by the way you behave, by the choices of what you do and don't do and how you do them. This is true of your spouse, kid, and so on. So you see, you do manage other people all the time. But sometimes you actually are in a position of authority or you have a stake in the behavior of the other party. And sometimes that party doesn't behave in the manner you wish or need them to.

So, if you are a manager in the workplace and have positional authority, or you have coworkers that aren't contributing at what you believe to be an acceptable level, or you have a spouse, mate, kid, or anyone else that isn't acting in an acceptable way, I believe there are four possible reasons for it. They are:

1. **Emotions**—that means that they are driven by their emotions.
2. **Conflict**—there is an unresolved issue in the mix.
3. **Negative thinking**—this other party doesn't actually process the situation the same as you, and therefore their motivation to comply is severely challenged.
4. **Performance problems**—this means the party just isn't keeping their end of the relationship bargain.

Distinguishing which of these is the root cause for the noncompliance is important if you want to really fix the problem. If all you want is compliance, you must raise the level of motivation through the use of something they may want or want to avoid. That is, bargaining, cajoling, threatening, and the like. The advantage is you get immediate results. The down side is you don't address the reason why something is amiss, and you also create a sense of entitlement for the reward and a sense of hatred or resentment for the threats. What you do is up to you, but remember the nine words to live by in "Of Albatrosses and Tree Stumps":

You always get a result from whatever you do.

That means, no matter what your choice in a course of action, there will be a result. What is important to ask before doing anything, is, "Is what I am about to do going to get me closer to or farther from my goal?" Then you act, and you get what you get. The more intentional you are when you act, the more likely you will get the result you want. So managing others begins with knowing what you want to accomplish and ends with doing only those things that bring you closer to it.

Cogito! There is an old saying (cliché really) that you can "kill them with kindness" if you want to make someone change. In a real way, it is very disarming to be nice and accepting when someone is trying to upset you. Isn't it hard for you to get angry at someone who is apologetic and trying to be nice to you? By being so nice and compliant with you, you can say they are managing you. Have you ever carefully listened to a good customer service rep?

You create many of the responses you get from others. The world in some ways is a mirror. If you want more people smiling at you, smile more. Manage others by giving them only one way to respond to you. Literally try it to prove it to yourself. Go to a shopping place and just stand there for a while with your relaxed, nothing face. Then deliberately smile as people pass you by. Make eye contact and maybe even nod your head in a hello gesture. You will see a very simple proof that the world is in many ways a mirror of you.

Relationships: When speaking with individuals within a couple's relationship (whether a love relationship as in marrieds, or business as in coworkers, etc.), I often hear complaints of how one maltreats the other. They go on to tell of harsh words or scowling faces and sometimes much worse. When queried about what happened just prior to an event or what posture or behavior they themselves were exhibiting, you often find that they are offering a type of resistance against which the other party can push.

When my son was about six, he complained to me that some kids in school would chase after him. I stood him in front of me and told him to chase me. He looked up at me and just stared. I told him again to chase me. He continued to stare. I asked why he wasn't chasing me like I asked. He then told me it was because I wasn't running! "Exactly!" I said. You can't be chased if you don't run.

Fred, a blunt and direct older man, was asked to develop a new way of handling requests in his department. His personal approach would be to develop it and then tell his colleagues what it was. His experience told him that they would resist it and likely resent him. So, in order to gain the cooperation of his coworkers, he started by discussing it with them and then gave them updates and listened to any critiques they had as things progressed.

When the time came to implement the new procedure, the coworkers were so a part of its genesis, they both accepted it and followed through with using it. Fred literally managed their change by choosing to treat his colleagues the way they wanted to be treated and not as Fred would have accepted from them. Managing the behaviors of others is a form of gentle persuasion and motivation.

This was a first lesson in how to manage others. In this case, you can manage the way people act toward you, in large measure anyway, by how you act or react to them. In an ongoing relationship like a marriage or at work, you can actually change an entire relational dynamic over time by adjusting what you do and how. The other party will have no choice but to adjust to what's in front of him and not the usual, practiced, tired, and annoying patterns of the past.

Of course, this is a prime place for your emotions to dictate what you do. For that reason, it is also a prime place to use your naked thinking skill of feeling less. Take deep breaths (surreptitiously, so as not to use them as another subliminal commentary). Walk away if you can and give yourself a few minutes to discharge your emotional energy.

Stay focused on what you want to accomplish. It actually gets easier and more automatic with practice.

Decisions: The value of this concept in decision making is selling your idea to others and getting them to buy in and comply. Never think in terms of the golden rule—that is, treating others the way you'd want to be treated. Think in terms of the better rule of treating others the way they want to be treated or need to be treated in order for you to get the result you're trying to achieve. The concept of abandoning the golden rule is very disconcerting for some and may require using your new skill of naked thinking, but it's necessary to establish the kind of rapport needed to motivate them to comply. Manage the way people respond to you by understanding *them* and then doing what makes sense in light of your objective.

TO STAY AFLOAT

A certain woman, Faith by name, awoke on a Tuesday morning as she had on every previous Tuesday morning. The sun was still shrouded by the lingering dark and mist of the Monday past. She dressed, ate, and started on her way to work.

As she drove, her mind drifted momentarily to what lay ahead at the office when she was greeted by the sudden pierce of a horn. She looked to her left and saw a fellow traveler passing her while grimacing in her direction and making gestures involving his arm, his hand, and some of his fingers.

As his presence became little more than the steam of his exhaust pipe in front of her, she began to play back what she had done and how the world is full of jerks … and perhaps she is one of them. Her stomach began to burn. Maybe she had had too much coffee and too little toast.

Upon her arrival at work, Jim was already waiting for her at her desk, a sheaf of paper in his hand. In a loud, controlled voice, he began to instruct her on the proper execution of her job. While he has no positional authority over her and indeed even worked in a different department, his harangue was deemed most enlightening … at least by Jim.

Once this training moment came to an end, Jim left in what must have been a hurry, because when he opened the door to leave, he pulled it open so hard it hit the wall behind it, and he didn't have the time to close it behind himself. Faith began to notice that her left eyelid was moving without closing. *How odd*, she thought. *Oof, there goes that coffee again.*

Around midmorning, she was walking down the hall to deliver a report—two days early, she was proud to note—when she met her supervisor coming out of her office. Evidently this report wasn't as important as the boss had led her to believe, and her being early was a sign that she had her priorities wrong. Having been relieved of the report and given what her priorities would be for the next three days,

Faith turned and walked back to her desk, where she sat and noticed that her left eye was not only moving but leaking now as well.

As it was now her lunch hour, she decided that she would go to see someone about this eye thing and how it was that her coffee seemed to be talking to her more and more these days. She went to see the local giver-of-advice-and-counsel, Thephil.

When she explained to Thephil what had happened and how she had reacted to it, Thephil read to her this page, which he kept in his knapsack:

To Stay Afloat

We are all born to live on the lake of happiness.

We are made to walk upon the water. Guilt, shame, and

criticisms are pebbles we find along the shore. If we pick

them up, examine them, feel them, then skip them along the

surface, all is fine. If we keep them, own them, take those of

others and collect them in our pockets, some day we will find

that not only can we no long walk on water, but that we are

doomed to sink and drown in what becomes a sea of sadness.

—Thephil

As she walked back to work, she took a closer look at her day and how she had taken the judgments of others about her as *truths* about herself. She had taken the criticisms of others about her as *facts* about herself. And then she noticed that she had not only filled her pockets with the guilt and shame handed her by others; she had been collecting them so long that they were as boulders in a sack slung over her shoulder, and she was inexorably sinking under their weight. But then she also noticed that she now knew it.

When she arrived at work, she wrote a few lines on a card and hung it on the door, facing her desk. She took another and placed in on her car's visor. In fact, she took many and placed all around her work and home and read them often. They said:

Just because someone says it's so doesn't make it true,
Just because someone says you are doesn't make it you.

That is when she emptied her pockets of the pebbles of others and what was left was simply … Faith.

Cogito! Everybody judges everybody else and everything all the time. Accept the fact that there will always be people who won't like you no matter what you do, what you look like, or what you become. Then evaluate yourself based on carefully considered criteria that define the person you want to be and let the rest be background noise.

Relationships: In life in general, we look to others' opinions of us as a benchmark or measuring stick for how we're doing. We also look to them as a means of judging ourselves as people. Of course, when someone calls attention to it, like now, it seems so silly, foolish, and downright unbelievable. We might even deny it's even true. But it is true.

We must have some way of judging our behavior in the eyes of others because in relationships, our behavior is far more important than any emotions or intentions we may hold in our hearts. No one experiences our intentions or love. They experience us through what we do. If we hate our boss and treat her with courtesy and respect, we may still have a useful relationship. If we fall in love with our coworker and treat her with courtesy, respect, and restraint, we may still have a professional relationship. It isn't what we feel that matters—it's what we do and how others experience us that really counts.

So, at this point you might be confused because in the story I suggest that Faith was paying attention to and accepting the judgments of others to her detriment, and here I'm saying we all do it and in fact really need to do it. It seems to be a contradiction, but the story clearly states the key to unlocking this paradox.

In the story offered by Thephil, it says of the guilt, shame, and criticisms from others, "If we pick them up, examine them, feel them, then skip them along the surface, all is fine." Here we find ourselves at a bit of a crossroads. Yes, we hear others' judgments of us, and we do need to at least evaluate the judgment. At that point, once our judgment of the judgment is made, it becomes our own judgment of ourselves, and we can now throw out that of other people. If that sounds muddy, let me clarify.

There are people we don't know or don't really care about. Some of them will give us judgment statements about ourselves whether we want to hear them or not. In most cases, it's best to just dismiss them as unimportant because they don't know us and they don't have our best interest in mind as they say what they say. So if a stranger at a street corner tells you that you are a short, ugly, ill-dressed toadstool, it's probably most useful to shake off your wonder of why they said it to you and just flush it down the ol' emotional toilet. That is one of the points of developing naked thinking.

If, on the other hand, someone important to you like a spouse, a boss, or a customer has a criticism, it makes more sense to hear what they say, evaluate what it means and how it applies in truth, and decide what, if anything, you might do to change what they're talking about. It is this step of evaluating and deciding whether to apply it or not that brings us back to the story of Faith. But once that's done, to obsess over it, think and think and feel and feel about it serves no purpose and pulls you down in that sea of depression, recrimination, and despair. Be open to hearing the judgments and evaluations of others in your relationships and then accept that what happens next really is up to you.

Decisions: Making important decisions requires a high level of self-confidence.

Who is relevant?

As a therapist, I have often had to remind clients that some opinions are more important in our lives than others. To determine whose opinions you want to listen to is a little tricky, though. Your mom may be relevant, but she may know very little about what you're doing, so her thoughts may not be the most useful. A relevant person must be someone who has insight into the issue you're facing and a sense of you as well.

For me, that person would be someone whose opinion I respect because I know how they form those opinions and that they want to help me be happier or better. In the end, only you can make that judgment.

Like Faith in the story, many of us find ourselves stymied by the confidence-cutting judgments and criticisms others level at us. Some may find themselves saying to themselves, "They make me feel this small" or "They make me feel like I can't do anything right." The fact is they don't make you feel anything at all. They say what they say, and it is you that either flushes it or holds on to it to use as a rolling stone on a snow bank, creating an avalanche.

Hear what relevant people have to say about your performance and your abilities. Evaluate what they are saying and find evidence that they are correct. Then use what you learn through that to make changes or reassert yourself as the capable decision maker you know yourself to be. If you let every opinion of you or your abilities ramble around inside your head, you will never really be making decisions; you'll be essentially doing the bidding of others willing to decide for you.

Training: The Infinite Loop of Cooperation

I've been a dog owner nearly continually since I was twelve years old. During that time, I've had the common need to housetrain them. This is a job I've always detested but one that can't for long be procrastinated. If you do, there will be a little bundle of motivation left for you in the most prominent spot on your carpet.

One method suggested is to always take the dog out at the same time every day. That is, the same hour and after the same activities. For example, always take the dog out after he eats, after you play with him, at ten in the morning, and so on. Eventually, he learns when he will be outside, and he then waits for those moments.

I had mentioned to a dog trainer that I was following this procedure, and he looked at me and said, "So, you mean you are now house trained?" I said, "No, the dog is." To which he said, "No, you are. If the dog were trained not to go in the house, he would not. What you've trained him to do is not go until these times. If you aren't home at one of those times, what will he do? He'll whine for a while and then find a nice spot to motivate you with. In other words, the dog will do as you train him."

Having been a people manager, trainer, and consultant for many years, a little light went off in my head when he said this to me. Most employees and family members act in the same way. If you "train" them to do certain things, that is what they will do. A prime example is a little girl that was brought to me for family counseling. Her name was Emily.

Emily's mom came to me alone first and told me that her five-year-old had driven her to the point of utter frustration. She feared that she would explode beyond her temperance, and she was tired of being the wicked witch in order to get Emily to behave. Her biggest problem was getting her to get ready and go to bed.

She told me that each night she wanted Emily to be in bed at nine o'clock. Emily needed to pick up her toys and bathe before bed, so she needed to start getting ready around eight thirty. But asking her to start at eight thirty usually resulted in a series of reminders from the mom and okays from Emily that went on for about an hour. At that point, the mom would stomp into the room, and then Emily would run like crazy to get things done, with screaming and reprimands going all the while.

She then brought her whole family in to me, and after a short conversation, Emily came over and sat on my lap. (Her mom had warned me that Emily wouldn't even speak to me since she disliked men so much!) We traded little tales, and once we were both laughing, I asked Emily if sometimes she is a pain in the neck for her mom. She said, "Oh, yeah!" "Like at night when she wants you to get ready for bed?" "Uh-huh." Amazingly, she was aware of the repetitive events and also upfront about it.

I then asked her why she doesn't get ready when her mom wants her to. She told me that she does. I said that her mom said that she has to ask many times before she will do anything. Emily agreed but said that she got ready when her mom "really means" it. I asked her how many times her mom has to tell her to get ready before she "really means" it. Without skipping a beat, Emily said, "Six!" Her mom's mouth dropped open, as did mine.

"Six?" I asked. "How do you know it's been six? Do you count?" "I don't have to. She says, 'Emily, Emily, Emily, Emily, Emily.' Then she stomps her foot on the floor and starts coming down the hall and says *'Emily!'* That's when she really means it."

Isn't this how you train your family members, coworkers, and employees? Don't we all do that? We set up what I call the infinite loop of balanced cooperation. That is, a static-state equilibrium of give and take that yields the result you want with a certain amount of effort. And with that comes a balance of responsibility for the outcome. For example, if you train the dog to go out every morning at eight o'clock and you don't take him out until noon, then you bear some of the responsibility for the little carpet gnome left as a motivational speaker for you.

There are other ways, of course. You could look at what you do until you're fed up and then stomp on the floor and scream "Emily!" yourself. If you have employees, people who you supervise or manage, children or other family members who you have an ongoing relationship of expectations with, take a few minutes to review how you interact with them and how they know when you're just saying something and when you "really mean it." In other words, don't get mad, don't get even; get more effective in making sure your expectations are known and that the others in your life know when you really mean it.

(For more details on effective communication, see the chapter "We Don't Communicate!")

Cogito! In our culture, it seems that we aren't taken seriously until we throw a lot of emotion behind it. When we say we want something, we must say it with passion or it's dismissed. The only way to break that cycle is to immediately introduce a consequence after the first refusal or noncompliance. Others will eventually learn you mean it the first time.

Relationships: In relationships, I call this infinite loop of balanced cooperation the Black Box Event.

Black Box Event: A predictable, co-constructed, repeated series of interactions between two people that is used for problem solving but isn't. It's used as a coping strategy in the face of some static condition that each believes they are powerless to change. It creates an equilibrium in which each party gets enough out of the situation to permit the relationship to continue at some level. Every ongoing relationship makes use of Black Box Events.

We train everyone around us how to treat us and what we mean by what we do. They observe us and experience us as we are and how we respond to them. Over time, their brain makes use of that information and begins to use it as a comparative for understanding us and a basis for deciding how to respond to us. The behavioral psychologist B. F. Skinner gives an insight into what might be at the heart of this phenomenon. He called it Operant Conditioning.

Operant Conditioning: Behavior that is reinforced tends to be repeated (i.e., strengthened); behavior that is not reinforced tends to die out or be extinguished (i.e., weakened).

In any ongoing relationship, we reinforce many responses to our own behavior by a variety of means. We may do nice things, get loud and even angry, or we might simply ignore the situation and allow it to die on its own. In any event, you are training others in your relationship what you really mean and how it's best to respond to you. Many parents have trained their children that "no" means no for a while, but if you whine long enough, "no" means "Okay, fine!" (Can you hear the kids yelling "Yay!"?)

Sometimes, these Black Box Events are useful and do a very important job. They can reduce stress, and they can actually help you through an issue with someone in a manner that can defuse it and allow it to move through the appropriate stages of emotional upheaval until the emotions abate and a solution can be addressed. But there are many times they simply set up a type of interpersonal communication that is cumbersome and even harmful.

Are you using this feedback system in your relationships? As I said above, all ongoing relationships use them, so you probably are. Look for them. If you ever hear yourself saying to yourself, "I can just hear him now … if I say X, then he'll say Y, and I'll say A, and he'll say B, and so on." This is the anatomy of a Black Box. Once you've uncovered one, go through the entire progression of what happens all the way through until you're on to other things and you're no longer talking about the issue. (That could literally take days in the case of certain issues.)

Like everything we've discussed, evaluate it before you do anything. Then address it by accepting and being okay with it, or talking about it with the other party (and this often requires the introduction of a consequence as a reinforcement for changing the behavior), or you can just change you and begin retraining the other party in a more subtle manner. Whatever you decide to do, remember that if you really mean it, you must never allow yourself to accept the old way of doing things or you will just train them to think that "no" really only means an eventual "Okay, fine!"

Decisions: In decision making, this infinite loop of balanced cooperation is most evident in the way we handle the tedium of going through the proper steps in making a good decision. As discussed earlier, it can be boring and burdensome to make yourself go through the processes required to determine the best outcome in an important decision. At some point, you may begin to hear your inner voice pushing you to take shortcuts and jump on the first thing that comes to mind. You get the conversation of the two angels sitting on your shoulders, arguing like the saint and devil so often depicted.

The fact is that we already have a way of making decisions. It works to some degree that is at least somewhat successful now. If we didn't, we wouldn't have survived this long. So your inner voice starts working on you, and you begin, over time, to allow the other things in your life (the tedium, etc.) to convince you it's just as well to do X as it would be to do some unknown Y you may never discover. This is your own personal Black Box Event.

Become aware of it. Examine it carefully. Sometimes the reason it wins is because your process of problem solving isn't really the best one for you. Maybe it really is too tedious. Maybe it is too cumbersome. Maybe it is simply something we put together because it looks really prodigious

How to tell your method of problem solving (PS) works for you.

One problem that Naked Thinking can help prevent is that of planning too much. Many of us get very excited, and before we know it, the plans for a simple issue become mammoth. If a problem is small, the solution is usually best fitted with something small as well.

If you find yourself laboring through your PS approach, cut it back to just the simple steps outlined in Naked Thinking. Good methods don't impress others; they empower you.

and important but not the most useful. After you examine it and evaluate it, treat it according to what you find. If your Black Box inner voice is correct, it may be time to reevaluate your decision-making process. If it's simply your little devil getting you to take a shortcut that might waylay you, stop reinforcing it by giving in to it. Remember what Skinner tells us; behavior that is not reinforced tends to die out or be extinguished.

LIFE'S A SELLING GAME

One of the greatest disservices a salesperson can do to herself is to disparage her job. Many are afraid to admit that they sell stuff for a living. The silliest part of it is that we are all salespeople—or we had better be if we ever expect to get what we want from others. A professor of mine from when I was in therapy school once said that if you want others to want what you want, you have to create an idea, buy it yourself, and then sell it to others. It all comes down to motivation.

Motivation requires three elements. The most important is that the people you are trying to motivate must see that there is something in it for them before they will be willing to do it. Notice I said be willing and not want to. This is a very important part of motivation that is often missed when the subject is discussed. If you understand that wanting to do something is not necessary, then you can put your efforts into what can create real results—that is, selling the other party on why it would be of value to them to do it anyway, even if they don't want to do it. In fact, they may comply and even commit for many years of cooperation with you and never, ever really want to.

Always look for what the other person gets from doing what you ask. What benefit is there for them to go along with or accept what you're asking? Is there any value to them at all? If so, how well have you worked to make them see it? All requests or demands on others have as an integral part of itself some expressed or implied benefit to the other party. Some argue that there are benefits and punishments, but avoiding a punishment is a benefit, so I simply call them all benefits, or more precisely, a value of some kind for the other party to act.

Often, we see a value for the other party in doing what we ask, but they don't see it. We also hear others tell us to do things when they see a benefit to themselves or us for doing it, but we don't see it. In fact, sometimes we will even ask the question, "And why would I do that?" The very fact that someone has asked us to do something implies that there is a value to someone for their having asked. That statement is worthy of a little more scrutiny.

Note that I said above, "The very fact that someone has asked us to do something implies that there is a value to someone for their having asked." Looking carefully at the statement itself, you see that, at times, the value to them is in the asking of the demand or request, not what we're being asked to do. That may sound a little twisted, so here is an example.

It's seven thirty in the evening, and Mom has just gotten off the phone. She goes into the bedroom of her daughter and asks her when the last time is that she spoke to her grandmother (Mom's mom). The daughter stutters and stammers with no coherent response. Finally, Mom says, "You call your grandmother tomorrow, and I don't want to hear any more excuses. Period!" And of course, the daughter will continue to neglect to make the call. So what just happened?

In the example, the benefit is only to Mom. There is no real benefit or value for the daughter (if there were, she would call the grandmother). There is no value to the grandmother (she didn't get a call from her granddaughter). So who benefits? Mom does in that the next time her mother calls and begins to gripe about not hearing from her granddaughter, the mom can say, "I really don't want to talk about it anymore. I've done all I can short of sticking the phone in her face and dialing the number myself."

Here, the value isn't really in the execution of the request, although there could have been. Just to take an excursion into family politics and motivation for a moment: if the granddaughter had called her grandmother, things might now be worse for Mom because it now shows that if Mom's mom nags her enough, she can get what she wants from her granddaughter. So it was really better for Mom for the daughter *not* to call, giving her legitimacy in blocking her mother's continuous complaining for a situation Mom can't control. It's all so elegant … isn't it?

There are people that ask or tell others to do things only as a routine of things to do. For example, there are those in the office where you may work who immediately want to schedule a meeting about anything you want to discuss. They may schedule a meeting for every thought that crosses their mind. Why? Because that's what they do. The value in asking for a meeting is to satisfy a psychological pressure to do what they've always done. When queried carefully, you may find that you can discuss and answer all questions right now and never have a meeting at all. Or that what they want from a meeting can be more efficiently executed in some other way. It is a prime strategy in time management to always question any meeting with anyone to assure that meeting is the most effective use of time in order to accomplish what is needed.

If you are a meeting person, you may find yourself frustrated by others that ask you, "What exactly do you want to do at this meeting? What is the agenda for the meeting? I'm standing here right now. Can't we discuss it now? Can you just send me an e-mail about what you want and let me come back to you if I need more explanation?" And the list can go on forever.

What the list of questions gets to, in the simplest of terms, is "What is the value to me for going to this meeting?" And of course, the mind is looking for the answer to, "Might there not be another way to gain that value for myself and give you what you want at the same time, in some other way—like not having a meeting?"

These examples are not meant to distract us from the point that we are all in sales and showing others how they benefit from our request is a critical step in getting better cooperation from others. The examples show how subtle it can be to lose sight of what you are really trying to do and how best to make it happen. The more you use your naked thinking and analyze what you're asking of others and the better you are at only asking things that make sense for everyone involved, the better is your reputation for being respectful of others' time, and you will be taken more seriously when you do make a request.

Take a moment and think about the people in your immediate work or family life. Aren't there people you have identified as people who will tell you things or ask you for things, way before there is anything solid to base their statements on? You know what I mean. Isn't there at least one person who, when he or she tells you that something may happen or asks you to gather information or meet with them, you are very slow to respond to because he or she has a history of saying or asking things before there is any good reason to act? Don't you say to yourself, "Yeah, right! I'm sure if I wait a couple of days, she'll come back to me and say, 'Never mind!' So I'll just give it a few days and see what happens."?

And then there are others that, when they come to you with a request, you jump right on it because you know he or she doesn't come to you with a request unless they mean it. Such a reputation is a cornerstone to being taken seriously and getting better results with others.

What if you do the analysis and can't think of the benefit or value to the other party for doing as you ask? If there really isn't any benefit to them for doing it, why are you asking them to do it in the first place? Perhaps you would be better off asking someone else or doing it yourself. Maybe you could offer them something in exchange. All too often, both at home and at work, we ask (tell) others to do things that hold no value or incentive for them, and the only value we offer them is that if they don't do it, we will make their life miserable. It's like the "Because I said so!" reason for doing things. Does this sound like your life? There are other alternatives, not the least of which is to be certain that you keep other people and their own motivations in mind before making any request or demand.

Remember—before you ask someone to do anything, and especially if it's important, ask yourself what their value in doing it might be, believe in it yourself, and then be a salesperson. Don't just tell it—sell it!

Cogito! Think back to a time when you convinced someone of something—anything. What did you do to make it work? Forget your fears and just do these same things again and again. Eventually, it will become what you do automatically.

Relationships: In customer service, there are two important questions you will want to find a way to ask as delicately as the situation would demand—and keep in mind that any ongoing relationship contains a customer service component, even a love relationship like a marriage. The two questions to which I refer are: why are you telling me about this; and, what do you want me to do about it.

As I note, you may have to word these differently in order to achieve the intended outcome. For example, the first question might sound more like the following if you are talking to someone who is angry or has a positional advantage like an angry customer of the people for whom you work. "I see. I can understand why you might be very upset over this. If someone did what you say these people did to you, I might be even more upset than you. But you called me. How do you think I might be able to help?"

As you can see, this question "supports" their being upset without admitting anything, justifying their being upset, taking responsibility for anything, or committing to anything. There is also the added component of being empathetic and giving them a moment to stop talking, thereby allowing them a chance to calm down and cool off. Now they can tell you why it was you they called and not the president or the CEO or your mother. In their answer, you may well find that they called you because they didn't know who else to call. You can now direct them to someone who can actually be of help.

Of course, skeptics might claim this allows you to dump them on someone else, but people often talk without thinking. Highly charged emotional states pressure people to act without a lot of thinking at times. (The whole point of this book is help you find a way to not do that, but not everybody will have read and followed this book as you are.) Occasionally of course, some are indeed dumping problem-people onto others. But it is far better to understand that person's needs and focus your efforts on the best way to meet them; often that won't be with continuing to talk with you about it.

Here is a prime example of when it's important to sell that person on the idea that you are not the right person to be talking to. Remember what was presented in the story—that you often have to actually state or point out the greater value or benefit to them when asking them to do something. So when it's time to pass them on to someone else, you can tell them why—and sometimes in detail, especially if they are really hot about it and have been transferred already to speak with you.

In any event, you are asking them to not talk to you but put their faith in another that you will connect them with. They already are talking to you. They want help now. You will need to convince them that connecting them with that other party is to their greater benefit. That's what I call selling.

In family, love, and ongoing work relationships, we tend to get lazy and just tell people to do things. If you're working with a person like me, it's okay to just tell me what you want, and I'll evaluate it myself and do it if it makes sense for me to do it. If my wife tells me to do something, for example, I may think it a bad idea for me to do it but a worse idea for me not do it, so it makes sense for me to do it. But telling me is okay.

There are others, however, who insist on being asked and not told. They want you to explain why. They expect you to show them all the cards in your deck of why you asked them to do this. If you are in an ongoing relationship, I would offer this: do not treat them the way you'd want to be treated (remember I'm good with just being told to do something); rather, treat them the way they want or need to be treated in

Example

Customer Service Rep (CSR): I believe I understand your issue and want to help.

Customer: Great! What can you do?

CSR: The best thing I can do is connect you with a colleague that knows just how to fix your problem.

Customer: You're going to pass me off to someone else?

CSR: Gosh no! I want you to have the best help we can give you, and my colleague will be the best person for that. I'd help you myself, but I'm not the very best we have for this particular problem. Hang on. I'll connect you.

order to sell them on the ideas you're presenting to them. Yes, it might take two or three extra seconds to do it that way, but in the longer run, it saves time and emotional currency and can be very useful in making that relationship even better.

Decisions: When you are making a decision that involves others, you will need to find a way to get them to cooperate with your endeavors. At some point, you may need for them to collect information or give you feedback or information they already have. You may need them to actively do things in preparation of the decision making. Then you will need to find a way to sell them on the idea of doing what the decision made will entail.

One of the best things to do in getting buy-in for a decision is to share ownership of the final product by involving the stakeholders at every step you can. The more they are involved, and that would include your informing them of your thinking and rationale for what you're doing as you go, the more they've already agreed before the final product or decision is made. In a sense, if they are involved as you go, they are already agreeing to the implementation as you go. This also gives you the opportunity to hear their objections and meet them as you go.

Selling your ideas still requires the elements of motivation, and the first is to make sure they see the value to them in doing what you ask them to do. Be clear. Be detailed to the degree they or the situation requires all along the way. Clearly show them how what you are doing or asking is of value or benefit to them. And keep this in mind: if you tell it, you'll get compliance; if you sell it, you'll get commitment.

WE DON'T COMMUNICATE!

As a counselor and consultant, I've helped many who have trouble dealing with others. One of the most often-heard complaints is, "We don't communicate!" They presume that if they do communicate, things will somehow get better, be better, and stay better. That might be true, and it might not be. Sometimes more communication is too much and can get you in trouble with the wrong person. But improving your communication skill is almost never a bad thing, so it is a good place to begin a conversation that might lead us to the true issue that brought them to me to begin with.

Write down at least three areas of your life where communication problems cause you trouble.

One of the first steps in improving communication is to realize that you are always communicating. That is, when you say you don't communicate, you are mistaken. What you really mean is that you don't communicate well or you are communicating things other than what you want to get across.

To be good at anything that includes other people (that would be working together, living together, raising children, etc.), it necessarily requires good communication. Here the word "good" means that you communicate what you want the way you need to in order for it to get the desired result. In order to be certain that your communication is as good as it can be, we start with what communication is and three basic rules of understanding regarding it. Let's begin with a working definition:

Communication: The transference of an idea from the mind of the originator of the idea to another. This can take place in any form or medium, such as hand gesture, art, music, e-mail, fax, speech, and so on.

What that means is that every word you speak, every inflection, the facial expressions (or lack of), gestures, whom you speak to and don't and when, as well as many other things make an impression and convey some idea. Believe me, you don't "don't communicate." As I said, you are communicating all the time.

This definition leads us to three important rules of communication:

Rule 1. One hundred percent of the responsibility for any communication rests in the hands of the person who's talking—that is, the person trying to convey the idea. Since a communication is transferring an idea from one person to another, only the person *with* the idea can ever know if the other party properly understands it. And asking, "Do you understand me?" doesn't really do it. After all, if they don't understand but think they do, they will answer "Uh-huh." And they will be very sincere but sincerely clueless, nevertheless.

Rule 2. To powerfully communicate at work (or at home), you must be willing to do so without interpretations, metaphors, and verbs of being. This is what I call "behavioral language." Leave out phrases like "you just," "all you want," "they don't care," and similar things as well as our dreaded F word—"feel" (as in, I feel you don't ... I just feel like they ...) These can be indications of mind reading. The only way to know what's really going on inside someone else's head is to climb inside. I've never seen it successfully accomplished and see no reason to believe it's even possible.

Also, we will want to eliminate the metaphorical language we use that really doesn't clarify anything. This would include phrases like "treats me like," "acts as though," "cutting me up," "putting me down," and others, especially with words such as "like" or "as." And stay away from characterizing the listener. Using verbs of being (am, is, are, etc.) says something about the other person, not what's going on. Note the difference between, "You are being rude (or a jerk)," and "I don't like the way you're talking to me. Please stop." One is about *you*; the other is about what you are doing.

Rule 3. The last rule is that you, the speaker, have the obligation (see rule 1) to be certain the listener understands your expectations, so it is up to you to clearly make them known. This is especially true if the consequence of not understanding and missing the point is great. For example, it isn't good enough to say that you want four blue towels. If communicating better is your goal, it is imperative that you say what kind of towel right down to the model number and the shade of blue you mean. If not, you will get towels, but there is just as much chance they will be the wrong ones as the right ones.

Keep these few rules in mind and live by them, and your communications will be far more effective. And remember, above all, never ever again believe "We don't communicate!"

Cogito! Every time you have any kind of contact with another person (that is through visual contact, verbal as in talking on the phone, written, etc.), you are communicating. Even if all you do is just stand there, you are sending a message. When you are truly interested in better communication, never be unaware of your posture, facial expressions, doodling, or anything else, because it will always say something about you to them. Make certain that whatever you do, it's what you want it to say.

Relationships: In an ongoing relationship, one of the most important elements is communication. As noted above, this means conveying your thoughts to another and receiving the thoughts of others in a manner that truly has them understood by you. Rule 1 is that all the responsibility for a communication is in the hands of the person who is talking, but if you want your relationships to improve, it becomes a requirement that you become an active listener.

That means you not only make the interaction conducive to their getting their point across to you; you actively do things to facilitate it. For example, if someone is trying to get you to understand something, help the person know if you do or not by paraphrasing it with the preface, "So, if I'm understanding you properly, you want me to XYZ. Is that correct?" This may seem stilted or silly, but it is neither. It is an effective way of avoiding a misunderstanding and a crossed understanding of expectations of what's to happen. When the stakes are high, this is critical.

When emotions are or could potentially become a part of the interchange, notice all the nonverbal parts of the conversation, such as the way you stand or sit, the tone of your voice, your volume, your facial expression (most people's flat or neutral face looks angry, so you may want to deliberately raise your eyebrows and nod while listening), and how distant you are to them. Never be too close when emotions begin to sour the exchange. It has a subliminal effect on the other party that leaves them feeling uncomfortable without their knowing it or why.

Use naked thinking to force yourself to do what is best for the communication and not worry about looking a certain way. If someone points out your handling them with your superior communication skills, acknowledge their being correct. Tell them that you are seriously wanting to understand them, and this is a useful way to be sure you do. Just tell them you want to get it right the first time. Offer to do or use something else if they have another idea.

Decisions: Communicating is less about the decision-making process per se as it is about the process as it intersects with other people. The above ideas noted in the Relationships piece are applicable here. The emphasis here, however, might include the way you interact when you receive feedback, information, or alternatives from others. For example, do you immediately flinch or blurt out a negative reception before the other person has even finished what he or she is presenting? Do you use phrases like, "Are you out of your mind?" or "What's the matter with you?" Do you immediately dismiss people without considering or looking like you're considering what they say?

This last question is a very important point. In order for you to facilitate the best communication with others, you cannot only be listening and considering but must show them, and they must believe you are. That means you must do things like nod your head, move your eyebrows, stroke your chin, ask a question of clarification, or any number of other things that tell them you are actively engaged with them. Otherwise, it might be inferred by them (rightly or wrongly) that all you're really doing is waiting for their lips to stop moving to say what you were already going to say before they entered the room.

WHAT IS FORGIVENESS, AND WHY DO IT?

During the course of a lifetime, we will meet people who range from so sweetly nice they nauseate us to those so coarse and crude they infuriate us. If we are honest with ourselves, we will realize that we will meet a complete cross section of people with a cross section of responses from within ourselves: some we love, many we like, a large number we are indifferent to, many we dislike, and some we detest. As human beings, there really is no way to avoid it.

Write your definition of forgiveness here and see if it changes as you proceed.

It is silly to pretend we do love, can love, or will love everyone. We don't, can't, and won't. In fact, there are some people we will avoid at almost any price—but notice I said almost any price. Herein lies the heart of this chapter. Are you avoiding some people in your life at a price much greater than you realize? Are there family members that you don't see or friends you rarely speak to because you don't like their spouse or other partner? What is the price you pay for this exclusion? Have you ever asked if it is worth it?

Some of us can say that it is worth it to cut a certain person out of our life because we can remember an incident when he or she did something to us. We might even remember a string of things they did that we did not like. But does your entire relationship have no more value than that? Is it so bad that you cannot forgive and embrace that part of the relationship that is important? The answer may still be yes, it *isn't* worth it. But what's important is that you ask yourself to make that evaluation—that you are making a conscious and thoughtful decision and not simply avoiding the emotional price it takes to get through the period of acceptance. Perhaps you believe that you did forgive them, but you just don't want to have anything more to do with them.

If you are neglecting an important relationship or dismissing an important person in your life, I challenge you to consider that you really haven't forgiven them at all. You've simply written them off and buried your ill will toward them. And since we don't like to think of ourselves as one that carries a grudge or the vengeful sort, we convince ourselves that we really aren't harboring ill will. Can you objectively evaluate yourself against the following definition and still say you've truly forgiven that person?

Forgive: To forgive means to accept (not approve or condone) that something you do not like has happened and you are willing to go on with the relationship without resentment. True forgiveness means that you give up all ill will and any claims to compensation, whether money or emotions. Since true forgiveness means to move on without prejudice, it includes a commitment to never bring the issue up again.

How did you do with your self-assessment? Are you really as forgiving as you say you are? In my experience, the average person has a very hard time letting go of a justifiable cause for anger and resentment. As a result, they may just ask themselves, "Why do it?" Why bother with the emotional expense of really letting something go? So they just write this person off as no big deal. But is it a big deal? If you have no further interest in that person or anyone they are attached to, such as a spouse, then there may be *no big deal*. But if you are cutting yourself off from an opportunity to love and cherish a rare thing in your life, a person who really matters, then the big deal is you are paying a very high price indeed.

Are you finding it impossible to make the decision to forgive or not because of family or social pressures? Here's what I mean. Many times in my counseling office, a patient has told me that they are suffering cruelties at the hand of a relative, such as a mother or father or even a sibling. I ask them why they don't just cut 'em loose and fugetaboutit.

They then tell me that it's just not right—morally, ethically, or socially within the family. To many, if it's a family member, you're *supposed* to put up with any and every insult and indignity no matter how bad. And what do you get in return? Just the knowledge that others aren't going to think badly about you for doing it.

Maybe you like your cousin, and everyone else in the family hates her because she cheated on her husband that everyone else loves. Have you ever been to one of those family gatherings and said you talked to so-in-so and then gotten shocked looks and derision for doing so? How about at work? Do you not understand why so many people hate someone (like the boss) and you just don't understand why? So you shun that person like everyone else, even though you really rather like him?

The decision to forgive is a personal one. All that is wrong with what happened is in your own heart. Give it up, and it's no longer wrong. All that will ever happen, whether you forgive or walk away, is in your heart as well. So, even if you ask others their opinion, the final decision is yours.

And what about the emotional cost? While you think you are over it by putting on the mask of indifference, be warned: it takes emotional energy to keep up anger, resentment, and hatred for someone. Do you want to spend what little emotional currency you get on such things? When you forgive and let the pain of insult and injury go, you aren't really spending emotional currency. You are in a very real way investing the courage it takes as seed money that will grow and produce a great dividend. And this dividend may be so great you don't even notice you've received it. I believe one great sign of true forgiveness is that you don't even think about it anymore, so the dividend may be that things are just back to the way they were, and you are now able to enjoy what was, before any of this ever happened.

Am I suggesting that you forgive everyone you have ever known that has crossed you? I suggest only this: take this moment to look at who is not in your life today but was in the past and ask yourself if the reason is that you haven't forgiven them for something that they may have said or done. Then ask yourself, "Is this the kind of person I want to be?" What you do with your answer may tell you more about yourself than you ever wanted to know. It doesn't take courage to love your friends; anyone can do that. It takes the ability to stand up to your emotions and make the right decisions about what's best for you to do, "to love you enemies," if you will, and make them again the friends they once were.

Cogito! To really let go of ill will takes emotional currency. But to harbor ill will and nurture it against the indifference of time and space takes a whole lot more. If you have extra emotional currency to spend on keeping up resentment, perhaps it would better serve you to love someone or dedicate yourself to a goal. But that decision, like all decisions, is for you alone to make.

Relationships: One of the great stumbling blocks in continuing a relationship is the accumulation of resentments. It would be a Pollyanna mind-set to say you should just flush them and get on with it. The problem, of course, is that people don't work that way. These resentments usually have a point of origin. Someone actually did or said something that bothered you to a great degree. At that point, you probably began thinking about it quite a lot and really grew it into a great big deal. Again, let's be honest with ourselves. It may really be or have been a big deal! That isn't the point anymore. The real point relates to the question, "What now?"

Either as a counselor or a consultant, we are often confronted with one or more parties to an incident that has created a rift in the relationship. In the workplace, this rift can cause so much anger, hatred, jealousy, and resentment it becomes the focal point of all the activity that transpires between them. That means the real reason for being there and working together (i.e., doing the job) isn't getting done.

In a love or family relationship, these rifts can cause estrangements and can set up the most elaborate schemes of avoidance and triangulation among other family members that the rift itself is now the center of family conversation. While this is happening, Father Time keeps plodding indifferently on and stealing what time for happiness you have without your even noticing it. The truth is people get old and sick and die. There really is a point when it becomes too late.

What naked thinking allows is for you to evaluate your place along the timeline of the relationship and ask if it's really where you want to be. It permits you to more dispassionately evaluate the benefits of letting this go or terminating the relationship altogether. What you wind up doing is part of that evaluation, and it may well be to simply let sleeping dogs lie and continue what you're doing, but it can also be the starting point for a renewed commitment to the relationship and all that's in it.

If you decide to move on with the relationship, one of the first issues you will need to overcome is the potentially awkward and awful feeling of your first steps with normalizing things with that person. He or she may not be quite as forgiving as you, and you might need to accept a certain amount of harangue from them along with a healthy dose of expecting you to grovel. In today's culture, this is very possible. Naked thinking—that is, clearly having understood the costs and benefits in your decision to continue the relationship—allows you to accept, not approve or condone, what will be the dues or payment for lancing this pustule and letting the healing start.

Remember this isn't doormat training. Do what makes sense. Agree or not to any prerequisites to continuing with the relationship. It isn't about being a martyr or victim. It isn't about being the bigger person here. It is strictly about deciding to take a step to improve a relationship you've already determined is worth it. If the price becomes too great, a reevaluation may be in order.

Decisions: Particularly in solving a problem with another person, part of the incentive for compliance from them may well be that they expect this to be the end of it. You may, for example, hear from someone, "So, if I do this, everything between you and me will be hunky dory. Is that what you're telling me?" The answer needs to be yes. And when you say yes, it needs to mean yes. Reread my definition of forgiveness above, and that is what yes must means. Without this and their believing it to be so, they will have little motivation to agree.

Summary of Section 2

In section 2, we explored the nature of what naked thinking is and looks like when applied to a host of different areas of your life. We saw that a great number of ideas that lead us to making certain assumptions, conclusions, and decisions are less than useful. Many are clichés that have been repeated so often we don't stop and think it through.

Some important concepts from section 2 follow:

1. **What other people think of us or what we do isn't necessarily relevant.** There will always be people who think highly or poorly about us or what we do. Love, admiration, jealousy, and many other emotions and motives can easily color the way people judge us and how they interact with us. Just because someone says it's so doesn't make it true.

2. **Time is of the essence.** We are often told that we can always pick up and start over. In some important ways, we can, but when it comes to achieving a dream or making certain that someone knows we love him or her, there is a limit to our time. We need to move up the calendar and have a sense of urgency if meeting a real goal is really important.

3. **Life is more than achievements and reaching your goals.** The best way for a person to be happy and still be motivated to take on challenges that keep up a sense of value and purpose is to find a balance of all the various things that are truly important. All too often, we leave out the most important and overspend our emotional currency on things that really matter little.

4. **Talk is more than cheap; it's counterproductive at times.** In "Fingono's Trap," we find how important it is to stay out of the realm of bluster and baloney. Talking about a problem can be helpful at times, especially when we use that talk to clarify an issue and fashion a plan of action. But talking about a problem

can also lead us to feel as though we solved something even though we may not have accomplished anything at all. It's a trap that can be avoided when using a naked-thinking approach to problem solving.

5. **The real power in your life is what you do.** When it comes down to it, life is a do thing. Whatever we might accomplish, it will require effort on our part to make it happen. Some things are problems for us to resolve, while others are dreams or wishes—even burning desires. But too many of these die on the drawing board because we just never get started toward making them a reality. A naked-thinking evaluation can not only lead you to the starting line but push you over the finish line if you're willing to act.

THE FINAL STEP: MOVE YOUR MOUNTAINS

Faith, it's been said, can move mountains. Without it, you won't even try. If you are trying to motivate yourself or someone else to do something, especially something as difficult as taming your emotions and focusing your thinking, there are three critically important ingredients:

1. You (or the person you want to motivate) must see value in doing it.
2. You must believe that you really can do it.
3. You must believe that the rewards are real and worth the effort.

In the chapter entitled "Life Is a Selling Game," we discussed the importance of seeing the value in doing something. Do you see the value in feeling less and thinking more? Do you see that much of your energy has been wasted by being pushed around by your own emotions or the motives and agendas of others who find it easy to access your emotional control panel? Can you see that the potential of emotions can at the same time be wonderful as well as dangerous and cruel? Do you see the value of critical thinking skills and deferred judgment as your greatest means of creating a life that is the ongoing source of infinite joy and happiness? If you do, then we've succeeded in our quest and found our way back to Kansas down the yellow brick road.

But seeing isn't buying. Element three above states that you must believe the rewards are real and worth it. You may very well see the value in feeling less and thinking more, but do you see enough value to change your life? Of course, I say yes. I do see it. As a psychologist and professional speaker, I've spoken to thousands of people whose entire lives are driven by their emotions or striving to look like it is driven so to others! Yes! There are people who feel guilty for thinking through certain problems without relying on their emotions. And if they say to someone that "they don't care" or if they can't fix everyone's problems, they fear that they will be thought of as being coldhearted. The fact is there is almost nothing more useful to enduring happiness than turning off the emotional fire hose and saving those feelings for the people and things you really love and care about. Never let anyone goad you into feeling guilty about not feeling guilty.

I was in Manhattan one day and walked over to a newsstand to buy a paper. The vendor looked at me and said only, "That'll be fifty cents." As I reached for the change in my pocket, I looked about and said to him that it certainly was a beautiful day, to which he replied, "Look, bud. If I had wanted to listen to conversation, I'd a turned this little TV over to *Oprah*. Just give me the money and get outta my face." I handed over the four bits, and as I turned around to leave, another New Yorker who was standing there behind me stopped and said, "That guy just insulted you! I'd have punched him right in the nose. Why did you give him your money?" I told him that I had written a book called *Naked Thinking*, and during that time of research and writing, I came to understand that it is not in my best interest to allow a newspaper vendor I don't even know, or anyone else for that matter, to decide when I am going to be angry. "You have a great day yourself."

Never let anyone decide for you what to feel or when to feel it. You are the master of your own emotional destiny, and you have as much right to feel nothing as they do to feel so much. It doesn't make you a bad person; it makes you someone who is more in control of your own life and more intentional in what you do. That's real power. And that power is the source of long-term, ongoing contentment and peace even when things aren't going as well as you might like. Use your power well, and you will achieve!

But let's not forget our friends and loved ones that remain in the grip of their own emotional traps. If we cross the great divide and look back to when it was so easy for us to get angry, hurt, jealous, hateful, spiteful, resentful, guilty, and so on, and see our loved ones on the opposite bank, we know that they did not come over with us. This was a personal journey. But as we watch how easily they are upset and how unhappy they are, how do we reach out to them? How do we help them? The answer isn't easy. There is an old adage that says the first step toward getting better is to recognize that there is a problem. Therefore, we must find a balance between being sensitive to their feelings and needs as they exist while remaining true to what we know and not allowing ourselves to slide back into a pit of emotional un-control.

The world is full of opportunities to get upset or get effective. The more you think and the less you feel, the more likely it is that when you take the opportunities presented, you will know both in your head and your heart of hearts that you have done the very best you could do. When it works out well, it will be a source of pride and confidence for the future. When it doesn't work out so well, you will be far better able to live with the results knowing that sometimes, no matter what we do, we lose. *And without the possibility of losing, there is no such thing as a win!*

Cogito! There is nothing wrong with feeling less and thinking more, even when it comes to dealing with the great social ills of our time. Don't let anyone push or pressure you into thinking that just because you aren't wailing and gnashing your teeth over the fact that you can't fix all the world's problems, you are bad. Feeling sad is something a child can do. Thinking through a problem and making intentional choices about taking action is a sign of maturity. Live well, do the best you can, be honorable in all your dealings, and you will never experience guilt.

Final Thoughts

The journey with *Naked Thinking* has come to its end. Like Dorothy, we have come down the yellow brick road to the doors of the Emerald City. I wrote *Naked Thinking* because this yellow brick road is real in our lives. It isn't a dream or just a story. It's what we wake up to every day; the hobgoblins and flying monkeys of life are real. But, there is more power in us than we realize at times, and the way to that power it to tame our emotions and focus the power of our minds. That is the entire point of naked thinking.

The answers to life's questions are not somewhere over the rainbow. They are within each of us. We just need to find them, face them, and embrace them with courage.

> May the sun stroke your face,
> The winds caress your arms,
> And the rain kiss your cheek …
> And may you forever bask in the light of knowing
> What you've done is the right thing.
> —Phil D'Agostino

About the Author

Phil D'Agostino, MEd, LPC-NC, is a licensed therapist in Raleigh, North Carolina. His practice has focused on relationships and mood disorders like depression and anxiety. His psychology education includes specialized training in and the teaching of cognitive-behavior therapy, solution-based therapy, RET, hypnosis, and conflict resolution. He is the author of *Ready Access CBT* (Cognitive Behavior Therapy).

Phil has operated five businesses, been allowed four patents, written dozens of personal development seminars, done three and a half years of talk radio, and authored countless articles for magazines and the E-Motivator. He has delivered nearly 1,400 presentations and consulted with hundreds of companies all across the United States and Canada. He continues to coach, train, and counsel through his center in Raleigh and has been married to his high school sweetheart for more than forty years.

www.NakedThinking.com

Thoughts and Ideas

Thoughts and Ideas

TRUE DIRECTIONS

An affiliate of Tarcher Perigee

OUR MISSION

Tarcher Perigee's mission has always been to publish books that contain great ideas. Why? Because:

GREAT LIVES BEGIN WITH GREAT IDEAS

At Tarcher Perigee, we recognize that many talented authors, speakers, educators, and thought-leaders share this mission and deserve to be published – many more than Tarcher Perigee can reasonably publish ourselves. True Directions is ideal for authors and books that increase awareness, raise consciousness, and inspire others to live their ideals and passions.

Like Tarcher Perigee, True Directions books are designed to do three things: inspire, inform, and motivate.

Thus, True Directions is an ideal way for these important voices to bring their messages of hope, healing, and help to the world.

Every book published by True Directions– whether it is non-fiction, memoir, novel, poetry or children's book – continues Tarcher Perigee's mission to publish works that bring positive change in the world. We invite you to join our mission.

For more information, see the True Directions website:

www.iUniverse.com/TrueDirections/SignUp

Be a part of Tarcher Perigee's community to bring positive change in this world! See exclusive author videos, discover new and exciting books, learn about upcoming events, connect with author blogs and websites, and more! www.tarcherbooks.com

TRUE DIRECTIONS

AN AFFILIATE OF TARCHER PERIGEE

Printed in the United States
By Bookmasters